P9-DNN-114

PRIVATE GARDENS

PRIVATE GARDENS

Succesful gardening in one hour a week

David Stevens

HENRY HOLT AND COMPANY
NEW YORK

LIBRARY
GARDEN EDUCATION CENTER
OF GREENWICH
2124

Text copyright © 1989 by David Stevens

Artwork copyright © 1989 by Conran Octopus Limited

All rights reserved, including the right to reproduce this book or portions thereof in any form.

First published in the United States in 1990 by Henry Holt and Company, Inc., 115 West 18th Street, New York, New York 10011.

Originally published in Great Britain under the title *Town Gardens.*

Library of Congress Catalog Card Number: 89–46423

ISBN 0-8050-1395-4

Henry Holt books are available at special discounts for bulk purchases for sales promotions, premiums, fund-raising, or educational use. Special editions or book excerpts can also be created to specification.

For details contact:
Special Sales Director
Henry Holt and Company, Inc.
115 West 18th Street
New York, New York 10011

First American Edition

Illustrator: Gill Tomblin
Line drawings: Sheilagh Noble

Printed in Hong Kong
1 3 5 7 9 10 8 6 4 2

page 1

This rectilinear tiled walkway is thronged with all manner of bright plants, some in easy-to-maintain raised beds, some in attractive containers, which can be moved to a suitable spot according to the season.

page 2

This Chinese-style structure, like the skeleton of a pagoda, frames a neat walkway with a gentle assymetry of geometrical forms, in the oriental manner.

page 3

A garden in the sky profits from the most exhilarating contrasts of soft and hard form, with breathtaking views guaranteed.

page 6

Overhead beams divide up a high house wall, providing a fragrant sun-screen for your outdoor room.

CONTENTS

Introduction

Good garden design is always at a premium, and it is especially difficult to find well-thought-out, sensitive schemes for small areas. Town gardens are subject to the vagaries of awkward boundaries, bad views, pollution and often a desperate lack of space, but this book shows how to surmount these problems and create gardens that are easy to maintain.

There is no doubt that an oasis in the heart of a city does much to relieve the tensions of a busy lifestyle. Bearing in mind that lack of time is a real problem for many of us, we seek a garden where we can enjoy the widest range of activities with the minimum amount of effort.

As a successful garden designer I create schemes for plots of every size and description – from tiny courtyards to estates of hundreds of acres. Such work takes me all over the world, but having said that, I started my professional career in the heart of London where the majority of my commissions were tiny urban gardens. This love of small spaces has never left me, and I appreciate more than most the intricacies of producing compositions that not only work in practical and visual terms, but also interpret that vital ingredient – the personality of the owner – which is the driving force behind all design.

Most people want to know how to start planning this out-side room. They want to know what they have and what they need, how to screen a bad view, whether there is room for a patio, pool, lawn, shed or any other ingredients that will make their garden both unique and attractive. This book analyzes specific requirements, explains the importance of a simple survey, and shows how easy it is to understand those seemingly unintelligible plant names. Above all, it describes simple and practical ways to reduce maintenance to an absolute minimum.

The examples have been chosen from successful town gardens around the world. Each one underlines the importance of a well-planned scheme tailored to a particular set of requirements. I have also prepared a series of alternative ideas showing how the gardens could be handled in an altogether different way. No two gardens are ever alike, simply because no two people are alike – which is why you should never slavishly copy a design from this or any other book. What this book does is to explain that vital sequence of analysis and design that can make a garden work for you, your family and friends. The world we live in is geared to 'built-in obsolescence'. It is refreshing that a garden is quite the opposite, continually improving in both visual and aesthetic terms.

ASSESS AND PLAN

It is surprising how often a glimpse of a tiny garden, backyard or even balcony can influence our final choice of a new home. For many of us who live and work in an urban environment, the need for a contact with plants and a little open space in which they can flourish is vitally important for our quality of life.

But a garden is far more than a place in which to grow plants. In many instances the city yard can be seen as an outside room. If you wish that room to require little maintenance, planning ahead – according to the guidelines set out here – will ensure your garden is a success.

Of course, in most instances the house has to come first and whatever you can or may do with the garden is forgotten in a mêlée of moving in and organizing the interior decoration. All this means that what space you have outside has taken on a mind of its own and – depending on the time of year and just what it contains – plants will have grown at an alarming pace. In many ways this may not be a bad thing; it can be very valuable to stand back and see just what does appear with the turning of the seasons. The old adage, 'more haste, less speed', is nowhere more appropriate than in

ABOVE *Walls are the essence of town gardens and their outline provides not only shelter but also the perfect vehicle for climbing plants.*

OPPOSITE *The division of space and the provision of a feeling of movement is paramount in any garden. This composition displays these characteristics fully.*

the garden. What a shame to dig through an apparently empty border in winter only to discover a wealth of bulbs and herbaceous plants just waiting beneath the soil for spring. These may have proved to be relatively labour-free.

This same 'take-your-time, wait-and-see' approach is valid where there are more permanent features. On a number of occasions I have had to restrain clients who wished to clear everything in sight before replanning the area. Not only does a 'slash-and-burn' policy mean starting from scratch, with all the additional maintenance implications that brings, but it can rob a garden of a potentially worthwhile feature.

One such example involved a quite tiny but sunny courtyard that boasted a splendid but huge prostrate juniper. The initial reaction was to remove the specimen in favour of additional sitting and living areas. In fact, after the space had been carefully redesigned, the conifer became a pivot for the whole composition, cleverly worked into a paving pattern that allowed room for all the other requirements. This garden offered minimal maintenance as nothing would grow beneath those spreading branches, but at the same time,

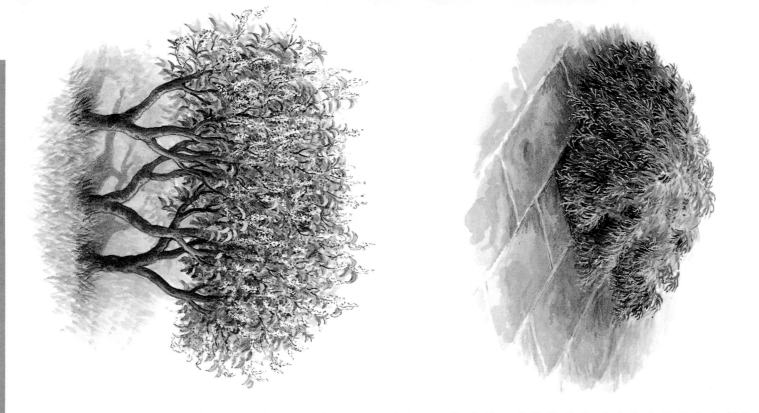

striking simplicity, which in the final analysis is the basis of all good design.

Another garden was one of several that had been formed from the grounds of a larger house, demolished for redevelopment. This particular plot had an unkempt hedge of portuguese laurel that divided the space on a diagonal, just over half-way down its length. Once again the owners' immediate reaction was to have the offending screen removed since it quite clearly diminished what was already only a small area. These particular plants were mature, displaying their natural tendency to provide a framework of twisting, sculptural stems. When the hedge was cleaned out, the lower limbs removed and some of the upper branches thinned, the result was a dramatic screen that divided the garden without completely blocking the view. The glimpse of the more distant space increased the apparent size and encouraged a feeling of mystery — that most important element of garden design. Such planting also sets up fascinating shadow patterns and the importance of light and shade in a small garden is another factor that is often overlooked.

All of this should go to prove that it is vital to draw breath before embarking on what is a fascinating project. It may be hard, particularly on the first fine day of spring when the local garden centre or nursery beckons with a wealth of attractive bargains, but at all costs resist the urge to impulse buy: it will lead to a jumble of unrelated features and plants, few of which will be easy to maintain and most of which will spell visual disaster.

So just how do we start to plan this outside room of ours and is it as seemingly difficult as many erudite writers would have us believe? Certainly not. All it takes are two simple questions: 'What have you got?' and 'What do you need?' — both of which need answering before any thought of a design takes shape in your mind.

ABOVE *Prostrate or horizontal conifers can be the most valuable plants in a garden with their evergreen foliage and ground-covering habit. Choose a suitable variety for town.*

LEFT *Portuguese laurel (prunus lusitanica) is a superb evergreen and a hardy shrub. White flowers appear in June and if carefully shaped it can form a most attractive screen across a garden.*

Garden Planner

WHAT DO YOU HAVE?

Measuring the garden is easy and fun. First draw the outline of the site and measure the length of the boundaries. It does not have to be to scale, but a sheet of graph paper is often the easiest to use. Mark the position and size of the house and the position of doors and windows. Indicate whether the boundaries are fenced, walled or hedged and indicate height. Draw in existing plants, trees or features that you wish to keep. If you have any paved areas you wish to keep indicate these also, together with type of material. Show any changes in level, indicating whether up or down and by approximately how much. Also indicate any good or bad views.

Now start on your plan using the check-list below to ensure all the points are covered.

☐ Northpoint	☐ Position of doors/windows	☐ Existing trees/plants	
☐ Changes in level	☐ Position of garage	☐ Manholes	
☐ Good or bad views	☐ Soil type	☐ Existing paved areas	

WHAT DO YOU WANT?

☐ Terrace/patio	☐ Lawn	☐ Veg plot lge/sml	
☐ Summerhouse	☐ Greenhouse	☐ Shed	
☐ Rockery	☐ Pond/pool	☐ Rockery with stream	
☐ Built-in barbecue	☐ Pergola	☐ Arbour	
☐ Bin screen	☐ Dog run	☐ Sandpit	
☐ Play area	☐ Swings/slide	☐ Washing line (type)	
☐ Soft fruit	☐ Herb bed	☐ Annuals	
☐ Roses	☐ Fruit trees	☐ Herbaceous	

ANYTHING ELSE YOU WOULD LIKE?

are you a keen gardener? _____ average gardener? _____ lazy gardener? _____

ages of children _____

any pets? _____

what will your garden be mainly used for? _____

is there anything else? _____

What have you got?

If you tell people they should carry out a simple survey, panic sets in with the thought of theodolites, ranging rods and men in yellow helmets. Nothing could be further from the truth. All that is needed is a little common sense and an appraisal of what actually exists within the confines of those boundaries. All the equipment you will need is a pad and paper, a long tape measure, and, if the day is dull, a child's compass.

Start by just drawing the shape of the garden out on a sheet of paper. Mark in the house, the positions of doors and windows, as well as the boundaries and what they are made from. This might be fencing of some kind or perhaps walls of brick and stone; in any event, check the height of these as they will almost certainly cast a shadow that will affect just what you can grow and where you are likely to sit. If a hedge surrounds the garden, be sure to calculate the width and how far it encroaches into the plot. It

ABOVE *Not all gardens display such a dramatic change of level but when they do an accurate survey and sensible design will be vital. This is a strictly architectural approach, tempered by planting.*

OPPOSITE *The view from a roof or upstairs window can be fascinating in town and it can be surprising just how green the city can be. It also gives you a bird's eye view of your own yard, often essential in the planning stage to give you an overall perspective.*

can be surprising just how much room this sort of survey, 'green wall' can take up, particularly when space is at a premium. Take measurements by running the tape across the back of the building and marking down the distances in sequence, starting from one side and finishing at the other. Make sure you do not miss any bays or projections and repeat the operation down the garden, starting once again at the house. Don't forget the seemingly trivial details like manholes, drains or an existing paved area: these could well impinge on the design later on.

Check the position of any existing trees or plants in whatever condition — we have already seen how useful these can be; identify them if you can, as this will make integration into the finished composition much easier later on.

CHANGES IN LEVEL

Any change of level will be important, so try to estimate this as accurately as possible. You can normally get pretty close by sighting back towards the house and checking the height difference with a tape. Remember that the thickness of a course of bricks is approximately 7.5cm (3in), so you can quickly total up the height of a retaining or boundary wall. If the garden is very steep or has complicated cross-falls, then the job will be best left to a surveyor and his fee will, incidentally, be worthwhile and will save your time.

VIEWS

How about good or bad views? Urban gardens are particularly prone to the latter which often consist of neighbouring buildings, with overlooking neighbours' windows. Ugly buildings play their part, as do most forms of city clutter — but just occasionally the role is reversed with a stunning glimpse of a steeple or an equally breathtaking panorama from a penthouse roof garden. Whatever it is, mark it down and try to show the angle or position of the offending or benign view so that it can play a part in the preparation of any design.

Roof gardens are a subject all their own. Such gardens are rarely easy to design, build or tend, but their inherent character in a sweep's world of chimney pots and roofscape can change one's attitude to living in the city. However, a professional survey is critical for a roof garden and a surveyor or architect should always check the load-bearing capacity of the structure below.

SHELTER

More often than not a garden is subject to a prevailing wind of some kind, or to turbulence caused by buildings close by. It is worth bearing in mind that a solid wall or screen can produce considerable turbulence in a supposedly sheltered area. This is because the current of air is forced up and over the obstruction, creating a vortex on the other side. Wind blowing along the face of a wall tends to accelerate, while even a breeze directed onto the face of a building turns down upon itself, often causing unpleasant conditions for both plants and people below. A slatted fence or permeable screen of planting can be far more effective as the wind is filtered through and the force is considerably reduced. In most instances, it is lack of shelter that prevents people enjoying their outside room, so if we know just where to provide this, then another piece of the jigsaw falls into place.

SOIL

Soil is divided into two basic components — topsoil, which is fertile and contains organisms and nutrients that help to sustain plant life, and subsoil, which is to all intents and purposes inert. Unfortunately, with many new houses and developments the topsoil is either lacking or was buried beneath the infertile lower layer when the foundations were dug out, and the resulting excavations were spread over the garden. Rather than try to improve subsoil, which is virtually impossible, it is better to have it removed. If topsoil is revealed then break the ground by deep rotavating; if this is not possible, get some imported. To grow plant material you will need a layer of about 30cm (1 ft) deep, but for a lawn, half that depth is adequate.

Should there be existing beds and borders, take samples, preferably from several different parts of the garden, and check these for acidity or alkalinity

OPPOSITE *A slatted screen is often more effective than a solid barrier. (Garden designed by Tim Du Val)*

BELOW *A solid seat that can be left out throughout the year is a real asset. Timber is a good choice, needing only an annual application of wood preservative.*

RIGHT *The mellow texture of climbers softens the boundaries of the garden and blends well with the taller trees and shrubs.*

with a simple soil testing kit or meter. This will tell you what is likely to do best, but remember that urban soil is often tired from years of being worked hard with little additional nourishment. A full test at a laboratory will tell you of any deficiencies and how to remedy them. Whatever the outcome, a good dressing of organic material will always improve fertility and soil condition.

SUN AND SHADE

The most important survey information I have left until last and this is a matter of checking what path the sun takes relative to the garden throughout the day. It is useful on your survey drawing to sketch the path of the sun as an arc, starting on one side of the drawing in the morning (east) and setting on the other (west) in the evening. This will help you trace the shadows cast by walls and buildings at different times of the day. The simple fact of the matter is that

we wish to know areas that are in sun and shade not just for purposes of sitting and dining but also for positioning plants so that they can enjoy ideal growing conditions. There are situations where direct sunlight is at a premium, a deep basement well, or shady courtyard, perhaps.

DRAWING THE PLAN

Up to now we have simply been gathering information, as much as possible in the simplest format possible. Before we can create a design we need to transfer this survey to a scale drawing. This, too, is simple and all you need is a large sheet of graph paper. Use a scale of several squares to a metre or foot, and plot the various measurements. Put in those good or bad views, show existing trees and plants and do not forget that all-important compass point. Once the basic survey drawing is complete, take several copies and file the original away.

What do you need?

Gardens, like people, display different characteristics. Those in the country tend to look outward to an expansive view (or at least one where the nearest house is usually a comfortable distance away), while a coastal garden is likely to need a degree of shelter from wind and salt spray. Town gardens, on the other hand, have altogether different characteristics. Criteria such as a desire for privacy, the elimination of traffic noise and the creation of an environment that turns its back on a busy urban scene will therefore figure high on any list of priorities. Some of these requirements will have been highlighted by your survey but others are down to personal choice and might well include ample room for sitting and dining, perhaps a small lawn if there is room, a barbecue, water of some kind, paths, storage for tables and chairs and play equipment if youngsters are around. Of course, the garden has to contain the functional as well as the beautiful, and space may well have to be provided for dustbins, the washing line and any amount of storage for items like bikes or tools. Include all these items on your check-list, and you will be able to see how they can best fit into the overall pattern without looking like an afterthought.

ABOVE A wholly congenial outdoor room in which walls are softened with climbers on trellises and the low-maintenance paved terrace is given incident and focus by a bold mixture of statuary and planting.

RIGHT Trees are the largest plants in any situation and they not only screen a bad view but also provide shelter and a haven for wild life.

GARDEN STYLES

For some, plants will be a priority to soften surrounding walls and boundaries, creating a soft mantle of greenery that brings a welcome breath of vegetation into a world of bricks and mortar. Others may want a more austere approach, using the garden to extend the natural geometry of the house with hard surfacing, wall colours and lighting. Both these approaches assume a controlled design, the one with plants, the other with architecture. A third option, and one that is gaining favour, revolves around a far more naturalistic approach where a garden evolves as a near-indigenous element, using plants that might colonize or appear spontaneously if the space was left alone for any length of time. Plants like buddleia and willowherb, clematis and elder would figure highly here, all of which would attract birds and, if room permits, other wildlife. Such an approach would form a natural oasis in the heart of a city and, with our growing awareness of the need for conservation, this approach is more than valid. Nor would maintenance be high, for apart from cutting back material where necessary and a degree of selective thinning to prevent any one species engulfing another, the garden would largely look after itself.

Of course, all depends to some extent on the amount of room available, and the shape and size of gardens in a city vary enormously. In fact this is one of the great joys of town gardening. Here houses, streets and alleys jostle for space, setting up angles and sight-lines that cross and recross. Gardens, courtyards, balconies and roof terraces are squeezed into the spaces left over, where the challenge of creating a living, breathing entity is all the more vital. In short, these small but myriad open spaces are the lungs of the city, providing room for us to pause awhile within them.

ABOVE A pergola should always have a purpose and in this garden the view is drawn down the path, beneath the beams, to rest on the terracotta pot. Any such structure is also the perfect host for climbing plants. Remember to check the durability of the material used.

ABOVE RIGHT Shape, texture and form all play a part in this successful composition.

OPPOSITE This garden is clearly both loved and lived in, the planting forming a perfect screen and being planned to reduce maintenance to an absolute minimum. Overhead beams define the ceiling, green walls enclose the area and provide a beautiful screen from the outside world, while the floor is built up from brick laid to a basketweave pattern. The line of the parasol is striking against the tracery of foliage and pattern of beams.

The design

In this sketch plan the priorities of the finished design have been 'roughed in'. This information has been gathered from our check-list and survey.

So by now you have a far better idea of what you have got and what you want. It is time to allocate space and begin to consolidate concepts. There is no need at this stage to work out a paving pattern or drawing and a check-list and, what is perhaps most important, arrived at an understanding of the plot's limitations in both physical and practical terms. A design may well be formulating and now you can start to produce a working drawing to translate that fact-finding into an actual outside room.

The first job on the way to that finished design is simply to rough out on one of those copy survey drawings just what goes where. The two most important factors here will be the position of doors and windows and the position of the sun through-out the day. There will, for instance, be little point in positioning a sitting area outside French or patio doors if you are a sun-lover and this area is in shade for much of the day. Far better to have minimal paving at that point and place the terrace in a position that enjoys sunshine, linking it back to the house by a path or hard surfacing of some kind.

That problem of a possible bad view will now be altogether more obvious. Do neighbours' windows look directly into your house or garden and, if so, how could this best be screened? The positioning of one or two small trees perhaps; the incorporation of a wing of well-positioned planting; or the erection of overhead beams or a pergola that will not only make an attractive host for climbing plants but break that intrusive sight-line at the same time. Another worthwhile alternative might be to con-struct a pretty arbour or gazebo that will act as a focal point redirecting the eye to a point within the garden. It will also provide screening and shelter.

If children figure in the overall picture, then the parameters shift slightly. There will need to be ample room for play, part on a hard surface that dries quickly after rain and is ideal for wheeled toys, and part on a softer background such as lawn. While the latter will probably be some way from the house, the former should be in direct view from the kitchen or main living-room window. If you threw that check-list of what you wanted open to the children then they might well stipulate a sandpit,

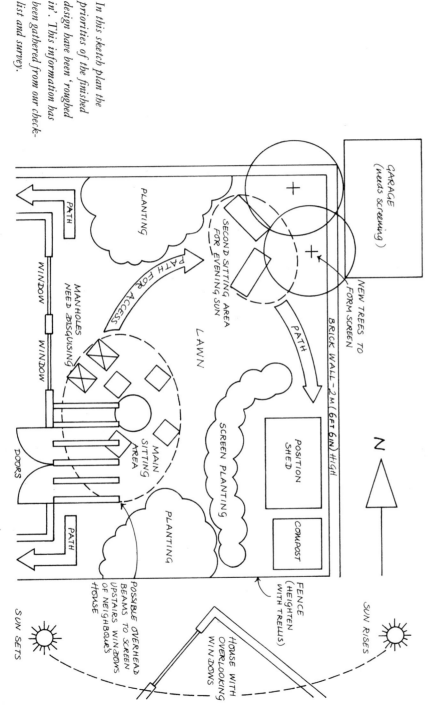

swing or slide. A sandpit, for instance, is ideally suited within a paved area, as the debris of a day's play can easily be swept up. Remember to fit a wooden cover that not only discourages nocturnal visitors but makes another ideal play surface. If the pit is raised with walls of brick, blocks or sanded timber, play is not only made easier but the feature can become something quite different in later life – a raised bed or even a raised pool complete with plants and fountain.

ABOVE *Many people are afraid of using a rectangular pattern in a garden because they think it may be too rigid and uninteresting – but it can be most effective. This space has been divided into a grid and the various sections filled in with paving, water and planting, creating different areas, each with its own character. Inevitably the planting matures to soften the composition and blur the divisions but the underlying strength of purpose makes a handsome pattern.*

WHAT WILL IT LOOK LIKE?

Design, of whatever kind, is largely pattern-making. Designers have no magic formula that conjures brilliant ideas out of thin air. More often than not they work to a well-tried set of rules that they know will have every chance of success. The advantage of a designer over a once-off amateur is that they have produced schemes many times before, eliminating mistakes by experience. Simplicity also figures high with a good design; a 'busy' pattern does nothing for a tranquil composition and is inevitably more difficult to maintain in the long run.

This question of being able to visualize the finished garden is important, and once you have roughed out the design in broad terms you can start to draw things up in rather more detail. There is still no need yet to specify types of paving or species of planting, but work out the shape of the patio or terrace, position the barbecue, allocate space for a pool, lawn and play area, marrying them together on the plan so that one runs smoothly into and on from the next. It can be useful then just to peg the shapes out roughly on the ground, using string or even sand to define the various items. Town houses are often tall and the view down from an upstairs window can tell you a great deal, virtually reproducing the plan you have on paper. This is the stage where you can alter things slightly. The sitting area might not quite be big enough, the lawn a little too long in relation to the width and so on.

To see just how to arrive at the finished design, look at the example of a typical, tiny courtyard garden. The whole plot measured barely 7.5m (25ft) and was dominated by a fine but enormous ash tree in a neighbour's garden. As a result the soil was impoverished and shade from overhanging branches considerable. The views out of the garden were nondescript, but at least it had the advantage of not being directly overlooked. The rear of the house also had full sun, a valuable bonus. On the debit side the space was tiny, and the boundaries were a mixture of fence and brick wall – the latter being particularly overpowering. There was no change of level to provide greater inherent interest and variety and the only access to the plot was through a narrow passage at the side.

(This question of access is always an important one when working with town gardens. Sometimes there is no problem, particularly in larger properties or farther out into the suburbs. Terraced houses, roof gardens and balconies have obvious difficulties, however, and in this sort of situation everything has to come into and out of the garden via the house, usually in sacks. This is not only hard work but can add to the cost of construction by a considerable margin.)

In such a small garden, with dominating boundaries, an attractive design solution can be for the pattern to turn in upon itself, focusing on an element within the plot and detracting from the immediate surroundings. This is precisely the approach taken here.

Near the house I have provided a generous terrace, spanning the full width of the garden. The materials are a combination of fine old York stone and brick, the latter helping both to soften the overall surface and provide a visual link with the building, which was also constructed from brick. The essential shape of the design is circular, the paving being matched into the circle of brick that in turn focuses on a statue or urn placed in the middle of the composition. Of course, brick is not the only solution and many low-growing, ground-covering plants could be used to good advantage so that maintenance would remain virtually nothing while providing a green background which is often preferred. Alternatively, a small area of grass can replace the brick but this could be a problem if it received a degree of wear, particularly by children, and it will also require regular mowing. If the desire for a lawn outweighs these disadvantages, or a ground-covering plant is used, it would be surrounded by a path to reinforce the strong ground pattern of the composition.

OPPOSITE *An alternative treatment for a small rectangular garden is to use a circular pattern, turning the design in upon itself and leading the eye away from oppressive boundaries. Here a composition of mellow old stone and brick sweeps around a central feature that could take a number of forms. Such a garden is really too small for grass which would quickly become worn and would also generate a maintenance problem. A seat nestles into the planting while the neat store caters for bins and tools.*

PLANT LIST
1 Fatshedera
2 Pyracantha
3 Mahonia
4 *Hebe pinguifolia* 'Pagei'
5 Kerria
6 Jasmine
7 Euphorbia
8 Cytisus
9 Phormium
10 Berberis
11 Passiflora

12 *Choisya ternata*
13 Lonicera
14 Hibiscus
15 *Fatsia japonica*
16 *Clematis montana*
17 *Hydrangea macrophylla* 'Blue Wave'
18 Arundinaria
19 *Helleborus corsicus*
20 *Skimmia japonica* 'Rubella'
21 *Hedera helix* 'Glacier'
22 Hostas
23 *Geranium endressii*

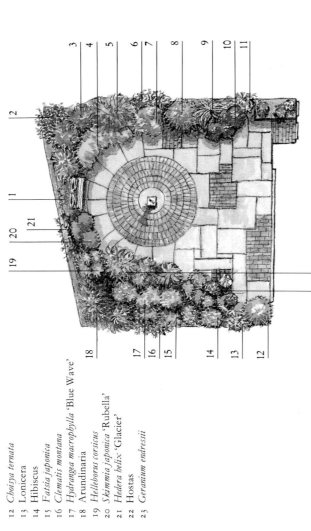

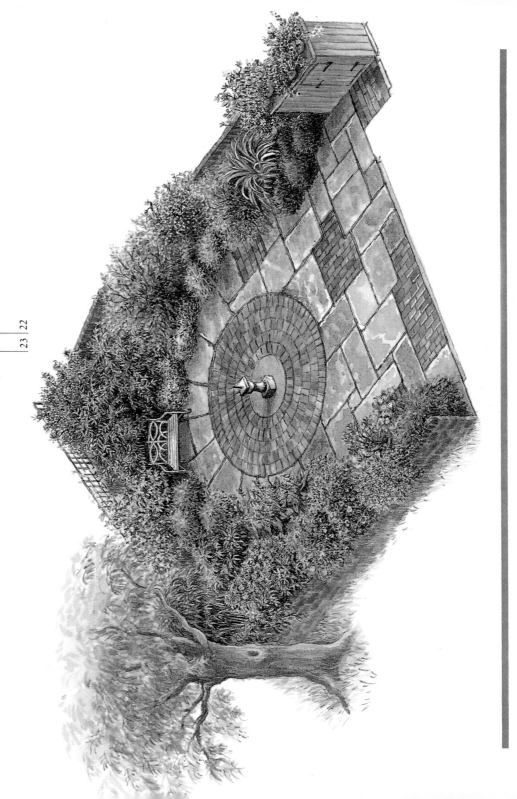

Additional features

This is a very simple ground plan, but it would be easy enough to integrate additional features should they be needed. For instance, if the garden was overlooked, then the seat could be positioned beneath an arbour that not only acted as a host to fragrant climbing plants but offered a degree of privacy by breaking the sight-line. To extend this theme further, the arbour could be linked in to a pergola that framed the path back to the house. The brick circle which defines the design and carries the focal point of a statue, sundial or fountain, is now as low-maintenance as possible. We have already seen that the brick could be substituted by low-maintenance planting or by the more time-consuming lawn. The easiest way to introduce plants here would be to floor the area with a combination of gravel, smooth boulders and plants growing through pockets of soil in selected areas. Such a composition would have a slightly Japanese flavour and, with perhaps a small bubble fountain incorporated, could provide interest throughout the year just as well as any full-blown planting scheme. Nor need the design be circular. This garden could have been based on a rectangular pattern, one surface overlapping and interlocking with the next with planting softening and surrounding the whole area. This approach is initially harder to handle in design terms but well worth the effort. Try dividing the space up, in the planning stage, into small rectangles. Allocate areas for paving, lawn, planting and incidentals like water, paths or herbs. Try varying the levels with raised beds or broad steps; you could try building a simple model to help you visualize how it might look in practice.

The other major difference between this room and the ones inside the house is simply that it is a living, growing thing. It is, of course, true that you can change and develop a colour scheme, rearrange furniture or purchase new fabrics and you can equally continue these colours and themes outside to reinforce the link between house and garden, all of which makes sound design sense. You should also think of using plants inside the home to link with those in the garden, but the scale at which you do this cannot normally match the space outside where subjects can develop to considerable size. This means that you need to do a degree of homework when selecting plant material, something that we will consider in more detail at a later stage in the planning process.

LEFT *Paving laid in a soldier bond has a crisp, no-nonsense feel that leads the eye down a path or through a space. It is interesting how quickly a well-planted border flops over the edge and softens the outline. It is also worth bearing in mind that when this happens a path needs to be sensibly wide.*

ABOVE *Steps should always be generous in a garden and this flight is well handled with a solid handrail and a straightforward change of direction. Planting links the two levels although the lion does not provide the best of focal points.*

PRACTICALITIES

A path around the garden will not only suit children but will make access to a shed or distant sitting area easier. Mark in the proposed route with a simple pencil line. Such a path may also act as a mowing edge, eliminating that tiresome chore of hand-edging and preventing damage to plants in an adjoining border from mower blades.

In a small garden a rotary washing line may be the most convenient. Position it within easy reach of the utility room or back door. If you are offended by its unflattering outline, make sure it is set in a socket so that it can quickly be removed and stored away when guests arrive. Another alternative might be a 'recoil' type that winds back into a neat reel when

not in use. While in this immediate area of the kitchen, think of allocating a small herb garden or plot for growing salad crops. So many people insist on tucking vegetables away in a dreary plot at the bottom of the garden, out of sight and largely out of mind. Many vegetables are delightful to look at as well as being good to eat. Herbs in particular are fragrant and often sculptural in shape, and can be freely mixed into the general planting of the garden. Plants like runner beans make a stunning display of flowers while something as good-looking as a globe artichoke should not be missed out of any garden.

Dustbins can often be housed in a neat store, either built onto the house or close to it with access from the kitchen. When designing the structure,

think of blending it into the background, using a compatible type of brick or timber cladding. The front could have hinged doors and the top be constructed to accept a range of pots or planting to soften the outline.

We have already touched on the possibility of certain components changing use during the life of a garden – a sandpit into a raised bed or pool, for instance. Much of this has to do with the passage of time and the growing up of a family, even though people tend to move house more frequently these days. There is no reason, however, why a basic ground plan should not remain constant while the components within it are modified to reduce maintenance to an acceptable level or to accommodate an initially cost-conscious budget that might later allow additions to be made. In this way a simple lawn shape might eventually be edged with a path, or the lawn itself be replaced with planting, paving or some other surface. In a similar way to the sandpit changing use, so might an archway between two different areas be used, first as a swing built from solid baulks of timber, with a temporary path around the feature, but later act as a host to scented climbers, the old path blocked off and feet re-directed under the arch and through to another garden room. Of course this type of approach need not necessarily be a phased development – such changes could be made to any garden at a given point in time particularly when taking over a new home and its garden. The ability to analyze the space, change it with a view to providing greater inherent interest and possibly substantially reduce the work needed to run it in the future is worthwhile in the extreme.

ABOVE RIGHT *A garden with children should make the effort to cater for them. A swing can be planned to be used as such early in its life but later on could become the host for climbers with a path routed beneath (see below).*

OPPOSITE *Although this support is essentially practical, it will provide a striking focal point later in the year. Climbing nasturtiums or golden hops grow well on those structures which are well placed in a small kitchen garden near the house.*

Front gardens

Because of the natural ability of a secluded garden to shelter us from the worst excesses of urban noise and pollution, we tend to forget that there can often be another area at the front of a property that is in many ways just as important, certainly in visual terms, bearing in mind that first impressions count. Here the space may be smaller, more open to view and more subject to wear and tear by visitors. It may also have to cater for off-street parking, a mail box, paths to the side and front of the property and much more. There is also a natural tendency to think that the space is not garden at all but just a nuisance left over between your home and the public bit beyond. Nothing could be further from the truth and, because it says a lot about you, it needs careful handling to exploit its potential.

The approach is just the same: survey the area, work out what you want and where the various components should go. Rough in the 'desire lines' which indicate the routes taken by callers to the various entrances. Don't be afraid to eliminate certain existing features: there is often no need for a separate drive and a separate path to the front door. These could be amalgamated into a single cohesive pattern. The choice of materials will be important to tie things together, while planting could be vital to provide screening from passers-by and soften the house and the garden's 'hard landscape' elements.

Sometimes there is virtually no garden at all — just the door and then pavement. This is the time to think about container gardening, window boxes and tubs. It is amazing how, with these, the whole façade of a building can be softened and made more welcoming. If you can, think of removing a slab of paving, providing a pocket of topsoil and planting a climber. In a few years a combination of flower and foliage could transform the most drab elevation.

OPPOSITE *The front of a house provides a first impression and this regular façade has been beautifully softened. In such a situation a climber is invaluable and if you can manage to plant it in the ground then it will grow far more strongly and need less maintenance than if confined within a pot.*

Check-list

- Have you carried out an accurate survey and prepared a scale drawing?
- Have you estimated changes in level in your garden?
- Are you interested in emphasizing a good view or playing down a bad one?
- Have you checked the direction of prevailing winds?
- Have you made sure that your garden has a decent quality topsoil?
- Have you made a rough plan of what will go where?
- Can you test the soil yourself for acidity or alkalinity — or do you need a professional?

- Do you need or have room for trees or pergolas to block a bad view?
- Have you considered paving, gravel or ground-cover planting as an alternative to the usual lawn?
- Have you identified existing trees or plants and decided which you want to keep?
- Have you calculated the position of the sun in your garden throughout the day?
- Have you thought about paths for access to sheds or sitting areas?
- Do you need space for sitting, playing, clotheslines, dustbins, etc.?

- Have you remembered to consider a front garden?
- Have you considered ways of minimizing noise pollution?
- Will you require shelter from sun or rain?
- Have you consulted your children about what they would like from the garden — for example, a sandpit, a swing or climbing frame?
- Have you thought about safety and ease of access for children and old people?
- Do you want to link colour schemes or other features between house and garden?
- Do you have room for herbs — preferably near the kitchen?

SURFACES AND STRUCTURES

The best gardens are designed with sensitivity, both to their owners' requirements and to their immediate surroundings.

For most of us the garden needs to fulfil the widest possible range of functions, as we have already seen. For it to do this effectively, you need to plan and construct the garden layout in a thoroughly practical way. Many a composition goes badly wrong because the planting is arranged at random, with little thought to an underlying structure or to the way each species relates to the other. Lack of a plan leads to visual disaster, laborious maintenance and high ongoing expenditure. For plants to look their best, require minimum upkeep and at the same time relate to their immediate surroundings, they need to be positioned within a cohesive ground plan.

Once you have looked at ways of allocating space in your garden so as to make the most of the site, as we have already discussed, you will be ready to think about structure. In broad terms, the structure of a garden can be broken down into 'hard' and 'soft' landscape. The soft landscape consists of plants, trees, lawns and shrubs, while

ABOVE *Timber can be an ideal paving material, if it can stand up to the climate. Solid planks of wood or railway sleepers have a natural affinity with planting.*

OPPOSITE *Steps should if possible be made wide and generous, making sure that water drains off them quickly.*

the hard landscape is the opposite, an architectural 'skeleton' of paving, walling, fencing and the other main elements that make up the garden's all-important structural framework.

A vitally important consideration of any design is the allocation of a realistic budget. Try to allow a sensible sum, remembering that in gardening, perhaps more than in any other field, you get what you pay for, in terms of materials and of labour. Because gardens, their basic components and those who construct them professionally have been undervalued for too long, there has been a proliferation of poor materials and a great shortage of skilled operatives. When you consider the cost of a good-quality carpet in your living room or the expense of a new fitted kitchen, then the cost of furnishing your outdoor room seems very good value indeed. It is also worth bearing in mind that the basic components, whether plants or paving, will in all probability last a lifetime and may well add considerably to the resale value of your property. You will need to begin with the hard landscape, the stage of the job that will take the lion's share of your budget, perhaps up to 75%.

Structures

The most essential priority which emerges from the survey stage of garden design is generally the provision of shelter and screening, so as to ensure privacy and allow the garden to be used to the full. In many urban plots these boundaries may well be in place, but in others they will need to be provided from scratch. Traditionally, builders have used local materials readily at hand for boundaries. If brick was the predominant material of the house, then the boundaries would be brick as well. Stone would be used where it occurred naturally. In areas where neither brick nor stone was readily available, you will often find concrete walls or timber fences.

Today, the picture is rather different, as a trip to any garden centre or builder's merchant will testify. There you will find a stunning array of both natural and artificial walling and fencing materials. The householder's choice often seems motivated more by whim than by anything else. It is small wonder

that many new housing developments display a jumble of unrelated materials, particularly in the areas of private gardens. It should therefore be reasonably obvious that the use of stone in a red-brick part of the country would be incongruous, as would brick or stucco in a city of granite. In many ways, the ease and relative cheapness of modern transport has encouraged such trends. Hauling heavy materials over long distances simply was not viable a hundred years ago and our cities looked the better for the resulting homogeneity.

But the fact of the matter is that we do have choice. While it is essential to evaluate the character of materials, their relative costs and the amount of maintenance required by each, you should also try to exercise a degree of sensitivity. A boundary has two faces, public and private. You have a degree of moral responsibility to make that public face acceptable, blending it with the locality.

ABOVE These granite setts have been laid in a strongly linear pattern that leads the eye towards the front door.

RIGHT In this garden, both surfaces and structures combine to break up the space.

FAR RIGHT These tiles, typical of many town gardens, make this balcony warm and welcoming.

Natural stone

Stone is expensive but, when used with respect and sensitivity, can be one of the finest and most durable materials for enclosing or dividing a site. As a general rule, a stone wall will only looks comfortable when its material is identical to that of the house, when it is likely to be locally quarried. In a city, however, where large areas can be built up from a mix of imported materials, this rule does not always apply. The scale of urban development often overrides intrinsic environmental conditions.

The colour and texture of stone can vary enormously, as can the way in which it is made available for building. 'Dressed' stone has been sawn or polished to achieve a smooth surface, providing a crisp, architectural finish. Blocks of dressed stone can range in size from unmanageably large down to neat, brick-shaped sections. Large blocks of stone are almost inevitably handled by professionals, using heavy lifting tackle, and walls are often constructed with little or no mortar. The end result is superb, but its cost can be astronomic.

The smaller modules of stone, however, are easy enough for the amateur to handle. Blocks can either be all of one size or or of random sizes. In either case, they look best laid in courses and, when using stone of unequal sizes, the larger blocks, or 'jumpers', can span two or three vertical courses. Always remember that many types of stone have a grain, much like timber, particularly the sedimentary rocks that have been formed in layers. Always keep the grain horizontal, as this will be more resistant to water and seepage and weathering. Stone laid with the strata vertical will break down more quickly, particularly in wet and frosty weather.

Real stone is indeed expensive, but there are many excellent reproductions, stone blocks reconstituted from a mixture of crushed rock and cement or resin. Blocks made from restructured stone cost a fraction of the real thing and can be used to good advantage either in their own right or, if matched with care, to repair a natural stone wall.

As a general rule, never paint stone – you will thereby lose the beauty of its colour and texture. If you are trying to improve an old, deteriorating stone surface which suffers from water seepage, use an appropriate sealer to prevent further erosion. Apart from the fact that painting is aesthetically wrong, it also increases maintenance requirements, as the surface will need constant attention to keep it looking reasonable.

Pitched face or rough-hewn stone is less urban in character, but would be suitable in a country town. Again, it will look its best when it echoes local tradition and can be laid 'dry' ('loose') or with a mortar joint. It takes an expert to build this type of wall, and if you hire a well-established local craftsman, he will naturally work in the style used throughout your region.

One great advantage of a 'dry' stone wall (i.e. a wall built without mortar) made from rough-hewn stone, is the creation of gaps and pockets along the face. These are ideal for the planting of small trailing plants that thrive in dry conditions. Such stone, because of its texture, also encourages the growth of lovely moss and lichens (except in heavily polluted areas). To encourage such growth on a new wall, paint the surface with yoghurt, milk or a solution of liquid manure.

Some types of stone are harder than others and examples of softer, eroded stone are easy to find in many cities. This is often due to atmospheric pollution, which can chemically eat away the surface layers of certain stone. Pollution also causes such discoloration that washing or blasting the grime from an old stone wall can yield staggering results: brightened colour and enhanced light reflection can bring a real benefit to a dark courtyard or basement situation, effectively increasing your garden space.

Marble, like granite, is a very hard stone. Its palatial character is usually too vibrant for domestic use. Just occasionally, however, in the context of contemporary architecture, a marble wall can look superb. Marble has wonderful reflective qualities, both in terms of borrowed light and mirrored images. Polished marble can be well worth its initial cost when it sets up glistening patterns of planting and people that is on the whole quite surreal.

Granite is a dour stone: hard, cold and unforgiving. It may be suitable for statues of worthies who embody these same characteristics, but it is not so good in the garden. Many Scottish towns are built from granite, which endows them with a certain austere bearing. Used with sensitivity, granite can be crisp, but it rarely engenders a feeling of peace and tranquillity which is the key to many a garden composition in an urban environment.

Other stones you may wish to consider are slate, flint and a number of lesser-known types. Each has its place in the appropriate style and setting, and all can be laid in slightly different ways to enhance their

visual appeal and make the most of their textures.

In an order of excellence, stone rests firmly at the top, even bearing in mind the high cost of purchasing it, and the importance of using it with sound environmental sense. If you inherit stone boundaries you are lucky – they will be worth keeping and repairing them, should that be necessary, will be a good investment.

ABOVE *Natural stone quickly acquires a patina of age that makes it an ideal, if expensive, choice for structures in any garden. Here it has been used to build a pretty raised pool. The wide coping has been carefully worked to emphasize the pattern and is broad enough to double as an occasional seat. Broad leafed planting is the perfect foil to crisp stone work and here its texture provides a delightful contrast to that of the stone.*

Brick, Concrete and Pierced Walls

Brick is the stuff of which many towns and cities are made. It is mellow and durable, and its small scale makes it attractive in a domestic context. On the other hand, brick walls are expensive to build and will need to be repointed after a time.

Traditionally, brick garden walls up to about 2m (6ft) high have been built 22.5cm (9in) – two bricks – thick, with a sensible coping or top course of bricks laid on edge. This approach is both workmanlike and excellent. As is so often the case, the simple treatment works the best. Today, you should still adopt this style, although you will see all kinds of other treatments, such as walls one brick thick with buttresses at regular intervals. This style is inspired more by the desire to save money than

anything else. While this can look reasonable, the coping becomes a problem.

Because bricks can be laid in different patterns – which are called 'bonds' – it can be used to achieve a variety of decorative effects. Whichever pattern you choose, it should ideally echo the construction of the house.

Remember that the foundation of any wall is vitally important. It should be twice as thick as the wall itself and about 45cm (18in) deep, depending on the type of soil.

Pointing, the shaping of the mortar joints between the bricks, will also alter the character of a wall. If the joints are raked back, each brick will stand out in sharp relief, producing a crisp, archi-

tectural line. Where joints are flush with the face of a wall, the effect is quite different. Coloured mortars, if used carefully, can create a pleasing contrast.

Whereas it can be difficult to curve a stone wall, owing to the size of each block, brick can easily accommodate a change of direction. Curved walls, which are called 'serpentine', are in fact inherently stronger than a straight run.

Concrete has a modern, no-nonsense urban character and should be used far more often in the garden, both for paving and walling. It can either be cast *in situ* which involves a degree of engineering, or concrete blocks can be built up like bricks. *In situ* walls are generally produced along with the house by pouring concrete into a cavity formed by boards. The best-designed poured concrete walls feature the pattern of the timber grain.

Concrete blocks have a rough-textured surface: these are usually finished with cement rendering (stucco) and possibly a coat of paint. Fairfaced (untreated) blocks can be laid with neat joints and left alone, a cost-effective way to form a handsome, durable wall. Because each concrete block is considerably larger than a brick, such walls are much less labour-intensive to build.

A rendered (stuccoed) wall is also relatively inexpensive to build, but if it needs regular painting to look its best, you may find yourself with a maintenance problem, particularly when fronted by planting. Rather than painting a rendered wall in order to extend a colour scheme into the garden, try tinting the final coat of render. This will give a more subtle effect.

So far we have considered solid boundaries, but there are a number of pierced or screen-type walling materials on the market. These are normally blocks about 30cm (1ft) square with a geometric pattern or part of a geometric pattern. Because they are pierced, they offer little privacy from the street and, because of their busy pattern, they must be chosen with care. Construction of a screen-block wall is well within the scope of the average home builder and maintenance is low.

If you want a pierced wall, but fear that the geometric pattern of screen blocks might prove too visually disruptive, a honeycomb brick wall provides a sensible solution and a pleasing end result, especially in association with plants. This involves laying bricks with gaps of approximately 11cm (4½in) in staggered courses.

ABOVE *If you are building brick piers, either to hang a gate or for purely decorative purposes, then always make them as solid as possible. Not only does this provide physical strength but it gives them visual stability that heightens tension and provides a focal point in a boundary. By varying the bond or width of the courses you can set up an interesting pattern.*

LEFT *Pierced walls can be both decorative and practical in that they can filter a prevailing wind and effectively reduce its strength. Patterned concrete screen blocks can look rather stark unless softened by planting. Such a wall is usually only one brick thick and may therefore need buttresses at regular intervals in order to increase its strength.*

Fences and Hedges

Timber fences are easy to build and blend well into any garden setting. They can be stained to a variety of colours and their appearance improves with age as they weather. Properly treated timber can last up to 35 years or more, and a timber fence will survive the shifting and settling of unstable soils better than masonry walls. Timber walls are also easier to repair or replace than masonry ones, though painted wooden fences entail more maintenance.

If at all possible, use timber which has been pressure-treated with preservative, at least for the boards or posts which are in contact with the ground. When working with pressure-treated timber, wear gloves and avoid inhaling the sawdust. Do not burn the scraps or off-cuts, and dispose of them in an approved tip or dump.

When it is not possible to use pressure-treated timber, an annual application of a non-toxic preservative (never creosote, which is poisonous to plants) is essential. This can be a problem when planting adjoins a fence, so leave a gap or, even better, a stepping-stone path that will allow both access and maintenance and tending the planting.

Easiest of all are panel fences, available in a range of heights and usually 1.8m (6ft) long. These are set between timber or concrete posts firmly sunk into the ground. In order to prolong their life, a gravel board should be set at the bottom of the run, close to the ground. This is the point most susceptible to rot and if this does occur, then the boards can be replaced rather than the fence above.

Close-board fences have vertical timber slats or wooden planks nailed to horizontal rails which have been mortised into upright posts. Such a fence is relatively durable and individual slats can be replaced should they become rotten. It is also an ideal background behind planting.

There are many other types of timber fence suitable for a wide range of house and garden styles. When making a choice try, as in other areas of design, to blend various features together. You can use irregular and rugged timber for a rustic look, or milled timber for a more formal effect. The bold horizontal or vertical lines of a contemporary building can be extended out into the garden by a crisp ranch-style fence using horizontal 22.5–30cm (9–12in) wide timber slats with a narrow gap between each. Such a fence has a strong linear pattern that draws the eye, perhaps to a specific feature or in a particular direction. With a vertically

slatted fence, the boards can be of any width and it can be interesting to vary the width of the boards within a run of fence to set up a visual dialogue, possibly with an adjoining paving pattern.

Nor need the timber necessarily be new. Old floorboards can be cleaned up, treated with non-toxic preservative and used as vertical slats. This cost-effective approach can look just right for the garden of an old warehouse conversion or as an internal garden divider.

Hedges fall half-way between hard and soft landscape. Although they are plants, they can also contribute in no uncertain way to the structure of the garden as a whole. A good, stout evergreen hedge can provide shelter, screening, colour and interest throughout the year, as well as soaking up a remarkable degree of traffic noise and pollution. Being plant material, they can be moulded to any shape, even clipped into topiary to provide a focal point from both inside and outside a property. A hedge can form a screen within the garden and in miniature it can form part of a lower ground plan, framing planting or defining a path.

Aesthetically, hedges are softer in outline than a wall or fence, which can be important in an urban area where you may wish to break the monopoly of harder surfaces. From a maintenance point of view, the species involved (see Planting chapter) will not only determine the amount of work needed to keep the hedge looking its best, but the size and shape to which it will eventually grow. Hedges do not need to be of a single type of plant; hedge species can be mixed to provide greater interest. Holly and yew make a good combination, as does a mixture of copper and green beech. If security is important, a hedge of holly, berberis or pyracantha can help to deter intruders and dogs.

Hedge maintenance entails both trimming and feeding. Hedges are notoriously greedy, taking considerable nourishment from the ground. In a small town garden this can be a real problem and even with regular feeding it can be difficult to grow other plants in the vicinity.

LEFT *This design is pure geometry and the strong vertical pattern of the well-constructed wooden fence works in direct contrast with the horizontal line of the hedges at a lower level.*

Trellis

Trellis is the perfect structure for softening the line of an uninteresting wall whilst playing host to climbing plants. It can also be used as a divider to partially break but not block a view.

Timber is a very versatile material, ideal for trellises as well as for fences. If possible, trellises should also be made from timber which has been pressure-treated with preservative – untreated wood will require maintenance and be subject to rotting. Trellis work is usually made up from thin slats of wood, plaited or overlapped to form a variety of patterns, and can either be free-standing or attached to the wall of the house. Trellis panels make an excellent support for climbing plants, can act as a screen across a garden and can form infill panels for arches, arbours and gazebos. The traditional art of treillage has had a long and distinguished history. Recently there has been a revival of this art and a number of specialist firms are now producing examples of first-class work.

Trellis made from plastic-coated wire is some times chosen to save money and maintenance, but such structures are on the whole too visually flimsy to make a worthwhile contribution to the garden scene. Rather more appropriate in a genuinely modern setting are trellis and arches made from strips of acrylic, which can look superb in primary colours. If you have the courage to extend this theme and paint downpipes, gutters and other architectural fittings to match, as well as using swirls of vivid planting, then the end result can be glorious, if eccentric.

Maintenance of trellis made from untreated timber can be a problem. You will need to remove plants very carefully in order to repaint the trellis or apply a new coat of surface preservative. The additional cost of pressure treated wood can be well worth it in the long run.

ABOVE AND RIGHT *Trellis can act as an effective divider between properties or within the garden itself. Remember that maintenance will be a problem if you do not buy pretreated panels.*

LEFT *Diamond trellis has a busier pattern than straightforward squares but it contrasts well here with the solid timber raised beds and sensible floor of natural stone set in gravel.*

Surfaces

Up to now we have been looking at the walls of our outdoor rooms, walls that define space, provide privacy and act as a host to planting of all kinds. Within those walls and to fill in the hard landscape picture, we need to add surfacing.

Such surfaces will, as we have already seen, provide the bones of the garden plan. In some small courtyards or basements, paving will cover the whole ground area. In other, rather larger compositions, paving will define areas for sitting, dining, storage, access and play.

As with boundaries, surface treatments can involve natural and artificial materials. Where a wall or fence is constructed from a single material, paving affords an opportunity to mix and match. Before running riot at the garden centre, however, it is a good idea to consider the basic design philosophy behind using hard surfacing. When choosing materials, you should look at the im-

mediate surroundings of the garden to see whether there is an obvious material that can be reinforced in the ground plan, strengthening the link between house and garden. The obvious solution would be to use stone paving adjoining a stone building and brick paving around a brick-built or brick-faced house. In some cases this can work very well, but when you create a very large paved area, use of a single surface can become too heavy and boring.

The answer can be to team up different materials, perhaps using stone to cover the majority of a terrace, but introducing enough brick, or other contrasting surface, both to temper the outline and to bring added interest.

Natural Stone

Natural stone is available in many forms: as the familiar flagstone slabs so excellent for paving, but also as cobbles, chippings, boulders and raked sand.

FLAGSTONES

Perhaps the finest and, incidentally, the most expensive paving is flagstone. It is available new, in crisply sawn pieces, or secondhand, when it has had its edges knocked off and is mellow with age. You can also find excellent precast concrete slabs which imitate new flagstones almost perfectly. The colour of the stone can vary considerably, from warm russet hues to almost black. Much secondhand stone can be dirty, and oil-stained slabs should be particularly avoided as these can 'sweat' in sunlight, producing a filthy surface.

Flagstones will acquire a dark patina with age, which means that they would not be ideal in dim or shady conditions, such as a basement or dark courtyard. The main maintenance problem with flagstones is the growth of algae, particularly in shady situations. This can be removed by scrubbing with a stiff broom and soapy water or a diluted bleach solution, provided that none of the solution makes contact with your planting.

The way in which the stone is laid will have a bearing on its finished appearance. Joints should be carefully raked back to emphasize the slabs. For a more informal effect, leave a number of joints open or omit small pieces of stone altogether, and introduce low-growing plants such as thyme to soften the outline and provide additional colour.

ABOVE Such a strong circular pattern naturally emphasizes the focal point in the middle of the garden. The sitting area is surrounded by a neutral floor of gravel which does much to tone down what is otherwise a very 'active' design.

RIGHT Broken stone and crisp rectangular panels are unlikely counterparts, but because they are used in a bold pattern the overall composition is striking. The white seat and planting are well chosen.

SLATE

Slate is a material of high drama – shiny, almost black and a superb contrast against a paler surface. Used in conjunction with surrounding white walls, drifting into a ground cover of grey foliage or demanding recognition against a pattern of white furniture, the result is both positive and perfect. Slate retains heat. It is a paving for bright places and is one of the few surfaces that looks better wet.

GRANITE

Granite setts are available in brick or half-brick sizes and were traditionally used for street paving. They are extremely hard, with a hard-looking, steely grey texture. When laid, granite setts produce a feeling of maturity in a garden and their small scale makes an interesting surface. It also makes them expensive to install. Owing to their slightly irregular surface, they are not always ideal beneath tables and chairs, but they can be ideal for paths, particularly on a slope or a drive where additional grip may be desirable. Small modules like granite setts can be laid in a curved pattern and this can be particularly useful to highlight a particular feature, perhaps around a tree, a circular raised bed or a pool.

COBBLES

Cobbles are often confused with setts, but are in fact round or oval water-washed stones. They can be obtained in slightly varying colours, from brown to grey, and are usually egg-sized. Because they are small, cobbles are expensive to lay and because they are uneven, they are uncomfortable to walk on. This can be an asset where you want to discourage people from walking, perhaps to stop people cutting corners. They can also be used in that all-important drive area at the front of the house as panels within paving to form an oil drip under cars.

Although you would usually embed cobble-stones in sand or concrete they can also be effective

Gardens more often have precast concrete slabs and pavers than any other paving material. They are inexpensive, easy to lay and form a practical, no-nonsense surface. They are available in an enormous range of colours, textures, sizes and shapes. With such a large selection, paving slabs can either be an inspired choice or a terrible mistake.

As with brick, the pattern in which paving slabs are laid can make a big difference to the overall atmosphere of a garden. A random pattern of rectangles has a lazy traditional feel, while stones laid to a rectangular grid give a crisp, modern touch. Narrow slabs laid across a garden in a breaking or stretcher bond tend to widen the space, while the same slabs laid down a path would tend to narrow it.

While rectangles can be a safe design option, other shapes can be more complicated. Crazy or broken paving creates a busy visual pattern which looks out of place close to a building, where it conflicts with the more simple lines of the house itself. It is more suited to the distant, informal parts of a garden. Remember, too, that it is expensive to lay crazy or broken paving well. Hexagons, penta-gons and circles are also difficult to lay in a comfortable pattern.

Paving slabs make ideal paths, particularly around a garden, between lawn and planting. You need not fear that this will lead to dreary hours of hand edging. The mower can run smoothly along the edge, which you will need to neaten up once a year with a spade or edging iron. Such a path also prevents the plants from being damaged by the mower. If using paving slabs to make a stepping-stone path through a lawn, be sure to lay them just below the level of the turf so that a mower can run smoothly over the top.

CONCRETE

Concrete is far easier to cast in situ when paving a garden than when making a wall. It can be formed to a wide variety of shapes and patterns. In order to prevent cracking it should be laid in panels of not more than 3.5m (12ft) square, with dividing strips of virtually any material – paving slabs, brick or wood strips – to act as expansion joints. The surface of concrete can achieve a variety of textures.

It is versatile, cheap to lay and good-looking. It is unfortunate that it is not used more often, particularly in town gardens.

ABOVE *These small precast concrete slabs have been laid with a strongly linear pattern that leads both feet and eye towards the doorway. Clipped plants at each side emphasize the line while panels of brick, set across and within the path, offer a change of texture and provide a more static element in the design.*

LEFT *Brick paving is superb, linking well with surrounding buildings and boundaries. It can be laid in a variety of patterns, this being basket weave. Always choose a hard, well fired variety that can stand up to winter frosts. The very smooth 'engineering' bricks look out of place in all but the most architectural situations and something with a little more texture will be a better choice in most situations.*

Timber and steps

Timber decking has a charm of its own, is easy to build to virtually any design and has a welcoming feel that you can never obtain with paving.

In more temperate climates, the main problem with building a timber deck is ensuring adequate ventilation below the surface so as to prevent rot. Use timber which has been pressure-treated with preservative or the heartwood of water-resistant species — such as cedar, cypress or California redwood — for any parts of the structure in contact with the ground. Timber decking is ideal for a sloping

BELOW LEFT *Railway sleepers are not only virtually indestructible but easy to lay provided two people tackle the job.*

BELOW RIGHT *A timber deck warms up quickly, can easily be cut to size or around an awkward shape and links well with a house built from the same material.*

RIGHT *Steps are generally for access but this little flight is used to emphasize the change of level and focus the view.*

site, where you can build a series of platforms — very effective in a small town or roof garden.

Timber decking also allows scope for incorporating garden furniture or other desirable features into an integrated design. Containers, raised beds, seats, fences and overhead beams can be combined to build up a total environment. Planting naturally associates with timber.

If you wish the wood to weather naturally, construct the entire deck from pressure-treated timber or water-resistant heartwood. Otherwise, the amount of maintenance required will depend on how you choose to finish the wood, with paint as the most labour-intensive and high-maintenance option available.

RAILWAY SLEEPERS

These solid baulks of timber can make fine paving, raised beds and steps. Try to obtain clean, splinter-free railway sleepers and lay them in a staggered pattern for the best effect. Being heavy, they need minimal foundations. Because they have been impregnated with preservative over the years and because they are so large, they are virtually indestructible and maintenance-free. When building raised beds, lay them dry-bonded like bricks and use a chain saw to cut them to size. Never stack railway sleepers more than three high without pinning them together with an iron reinforcing rod. When working with railway sleepers, wear gloves to guard against splinters and avoid breathing the sawdust.

A change of level can add an attractive dimension to almost any garden, but bad handling can mar a composition. As a general rule, a gentle slope should be terraced in broad sections to reinforce an underlying feeling of stability. Steps, or more occasionally ramps, are best for linking different levels. These can be built in a material to match those used in other parts of the garden, but it can be a good idea to emphasize the position of the steps by a change in paving pattern or in paving material, particularly if it is not obvious that steps are ahead. A course of brick set at the top of a flight of flagstones will just act as a visual warning.

As a general rule, the more generous the flight, the better. There is nothing worse, or more danger-ous, than a mean set of steps. The treads should be at least 45 cm (18 in) deep and virtually as wide as you like; the risers should be approximately 15 cm (6 in). In some cases, a series of steps can become plat-forms or terraces in their own right. If the garden is small, such terraced steps can fill the entire space, accommodating all the furnishings that cater for living outside.

Steps, whether large or small, can be any shape — semi-circular, straight, interlocking, hexagonal — but their shape should directly relate to the overall design of the garden. Within your design, you will find steps particularly useful to achieve a change of direction, turning the feet and the eye from one point to the next.

Features

When the main aspects of the garden have been resolved — the boundaries and surface — and compatible materials chosen, you can look at the features that will personalize the composition.

Raised beds can be a real asset. They should be constructed to accept the weight of the soil in them and incorporate drainage to prevent waterlogging. Beds of different heights and sizes can interlock, and might incorporate steps, built-in seating or even a water feature. Such beds lift plants to eye level and ease maintenance, as there is no need to stoop. Raised timber beds in a roof garden are particularly useful; use lightweight soil to reduce the load on the structure below.

GARDEN BUILDINGS

Buildings in a garden come in two types, decorative — gazebos, summerhouses, and pavilions — and utility — greenhouses, storerooms and workshops.

Most town gardens are too small to include both, so a utility building should also be decorative. If you want something worthwhile, seek inspiration from gardening books of the early 1900s. However, do not allow garden buildings to dominate: any structure should be just one part of the design.

Pergolas, arbours and arches are ideal in town to act as screens and to divide the garden. They can be the perfect vehicle for climbing plants, while the simple arches can emphasize the different areas.

A pergola is a series of extended arches and should always have somewhere to go. It could finish nowhere better than at an arbour, an open structure of beams that forms a canopy over a sitting area. An arbour can either abut a wall or be free-standing; smothered with fragrant climbers, it provides the perfect shady retreat from the midday sun.

All these features involve a degree of work in maintaining the structure and the climbing plants trained over them (see Labour-Saving chapter). With proper construction and modern pressure-treated timber, this can be kept to a minimum.

WATER

In an urban garden, any pond or pool is likely to be of modest size. Stick to simple rectangular shapes and use planting to soften the outline and blend water into the outer surfaces. Consider how sight-lines will affect the composition, not forgetting plants and statues. The smaller the pool, the simpler it should be in shape and design.

Check-list

- Have you worked out a realistic budget? – bear in mind that a short-term economy can cost a lot more in the long run.

- Have you made an initial decision on what kind of boundary you want – hard, soft, or a combination of the two?

- For your hard boundary, have you made a considered choice from the many types and arrangements of natural stone, brick, concrete and timber?

- Have you considered softening your hard boundary, using climbing plants and hedging?

- Do you need a dividing screen or a lighter boundary? – consider trellis, pierced wall or hedging

- Choose your surface: do you want it to blend, or contrast with your boundaries?

- Do you need a flight of steps, terracing, or raised beds to accommodate a change of level?

- Would your garden benefit from overhead structures, to break up a high house wall, or a garden building?

Water provides a focal point in any garden. In this situation a net spread over the surface when leaves fall in autumn would save considerable maintenance.

LOW-MAINTENANCE PLANTING

For most people the planting is the garden – it brings a carefully considered and constructed framework to life. Nonetheless, the subject of planting engenders vast and mystifying confusion. More often than not, it is this aspect of gardening that initially seems to be the most difficult to handle. This is due in part to the daunting prospect of mastering long lists of Latin plant names. Then there is the fact that plants all grow to different heights or spread to different widths; some are deciduous, shedding their leaves in the winter, while others are evergreen; and they all flower at different times of the year.

The spectre of a few sparsely planted shrubs awash in a sea of labour-intensive weeds is more than enough to deter even the most intrepid from starting. Fortunately, this is a problem that can be easily avoided. All of the planting recommendations in this book require little maintenance. With experience and planning you will naturally discover many others. You will find, for instance, that seasonal planting is more labour-intensive than planting permanent shrubs, climbers and hardy perennials. The way to a well-planted and virtually maintenance-free garden is, in fact, far from complicated. As with the earlier stages of the garden design, take your time and plan your planting. Buying plants on impulse from your local garden centre or accepting a flood of well-meant cuttings from family and neighbours is almost certain to spell disaster. Look carefully through some good plant dictionaries. Take the time to observe carefully public gardens or friends'

plots that you particularly admire. Don't be afraid to jot names down or to ask questions – knowledgeable gardeners part with information easily and are very glad to give help and advice.

Plants range in shape and size from the obvious bulk of a tree down to the tiny leaves of grass that form a lawn. If you look at the 'planting' of a natural environment – oak woodland, for instance – you will see that the plants are grouped in layers. Trees form the highest storey, followed by a layer of shrubs, with sprawling ground cover at the lowest level. A wood may appear untidy to the untrained eye, but it needs little maintenance unless specifically meddled with by man. The garden is a more controlled situation, but the same basic structure must exist and the same basic principles must be applied.

When working out a planting plan, the first job is to select tough, largely evergreen material to form a background and provide shelter and screening. Such plants – indeed all plants – must be chosen for their suitability to the specific environment where they are to grow. Do you need a plant which thrives in sun or shade? One which can tolerate a specific type of soil or particularly high levels of pollution? Rapid development may well be important too, and for this you could consider shrubs such as arundinaria, fatsia, elaeagnus, viburnum, mahonia, choisya or kerria. Some shrubs such as ligustrum or forsythia might be altogether too large for a small plot.

The way in which plants are grouped is also important. A garden full of single specimens is

ABOVE Every composition should display colour and interest throughout the year as well as keeping maintenance to a sensible minimum. Here hostas are ideal ground cover; they also display a sculptural leaf pattern which can be as eye-catching as any flower.

OPPOSITE Plants bring a garden to life and here there is a subtle contrast of form and foliage that leads the eye towards the shady doorway, emphasized by the spiral bay tree. This largely evergreen display would ensure interest throughout the year.

naturally restless, leading the eye to jump from one species to the next with little continuity. Background planting should be carried out in groups of two or three, even in a small garden, with the odd single specimen included for emphasis. Once this main framework of plants is in position, you can start to fill in the intermediate areas between main plants with smaller, lighter and altogether more colourful material: herbaceous plants (also known as hardy perennials) and smaller shrubs. The range of shrubs available is enormous, as any good directory will show, and you should choose ones which will grow to about 1m (3–4ft) high, such as varieties of spiraea, potentilla, fuchsia, senecio, rosmarinus and hypericum. Sturdy shrubs can help support herbaceous plants which might otherwise require tedious staking and tying.

Herbaceous plants inject colour and their fast growth makes them ideal for linking ranges of shrubs together. Plant them in groups of six, eight or a dozen, depending on their eventual size. Such groups can lead the eye through a bed or around a corner, providing a feeling of space and movement.

Ground cover is the lowest layer, underplanting the other species and reducing maintenance to an absolute minimum if correctly chosen. Plants for this purpose should have a spreading habit of growth and most will be naturally ground-hugging.

Here you will find an ample choice of species to suit any conditions, whether it be sun, shade, damp, or a specific soil type. Some climbing plants form excellent ground cover and will also naturally grow up any wall or obstacle: try ivy (hedera), honeysuckle (lonicera) and the climbing *Hydrangea anomala* subsp. *petiolaris*. Ground cover plants can be used in considerable numbers to form bold drifts, depending on the eventual size of the plant you choose, and groupings of up to fifty plants in even a quite small garden could be acceptable.

Grass could be described as an excellent ground cover. In terms of maintenance, the upkeep of a grassed area is not difficult, simply regular. Weeds can be controlled simply with an annual application of a combination fertilizer and weedkiller. A well-designed garden has a lawn that is shaped to allow easy access to all parts with a mower and probably incorporates a surrounding path or brick edge that eliminates the tiresome chore of hand-edging.

After considering the overall structure of plant-ing, the next element to consider for each plant is its time of flowering and the colour of its bloom, berries or foliage. Colour co-ordination may seem a daunting task, but there are a few simple guidelines. Always remember that vibrant, hot colours, such as bright red, orange and lemon yellow, tend to draw the eye. This can mean that hot colours foreshorten a space when they are grouped some distance away from a viewpoint. In other words, such colours will almost certainly look best relatively close to the house. The softer blues, pinks, purples and, of course, white, should lead away into the further parts of the garden. Grey is a great harmonizer in most design situations, with its ability to link and tie colour ranges together.

So, when you are deciding how to arrange the plants in your garden, be sure to carry out a degree of interesting and really vital research beforehand.

Planting design may be one of the more demanding aspects of garden planning, but it is both worthwhile and rewarding.

LEFT *The circular movement of this garden is echoed in the planting of the beds. The rich evergreens are an ideal counterpoint to the harsh paving and the colour themes are continuous throughout.*

BELOW *Planting design is all about juxtaposition, and as here, the foliage of a plant is often more important than a flush of flower. This is the perfect example of a luxuriant contrast of many different heights, colours and textures. Iris, onopordum, ligularia and rheum combine in a delightful harmony of forms, in which one could constantly find new shapes and textures to admire.*

Ground cover

Gardening, like any other pastime, is subject to the whims of fashion and ground cover has been hailed in recent years as a most significant part of good gardening. In fact, plants which carpet the ground and thereby reduce maintenance to a minimum have always been with us, both in natural landscapes and in the garden. The real value of ground cover as a labour-saver became evident when the age of the hired hand came to an end, and as a result it has been with us ever since.

There is a ground cover plant for every situation – sun, shade or bog, as well as acid or alkaline soil. Many bear attractive flowers and, because they grow so densely, the blooms are usually profuse. Evergreen types are particularly useful. Although you naturally assume that ground cover plants are fairly small, the real criterion is that they should hug the ground or have foliage so dense that it excludes other growth beneath. Some quite large shrubs fall into this category, including types of rhododendron, aucuba and mahonia. These species would only be planted singly or in small groups, but the low, ground-hugging types should be used in bold drifts of several dozen or more.

Many plants have the characteristic growth pattern needed for ground cover: a tendency to spread, grow together and form clumps or mats. Some are far too rampant to let loose in the garden and are normally called weeds. Ground elder is an excellent example: invasive, dominant, but a perfect carpeter if allowed to run in an enclosed area. There is, incidentally, a variegated form that is rather less invasive and just about suitable for the garden. Some people would put *Hypericum calycinum* (Rose of Sharon) in the same class, but this can be an invaluable plant in both sun and shade, bearing bright, buttercup flowers and a wealth of evergreen foliage. It is best to check just how strong a grower the plant really is and position it within the scheme accordingly. The real demons can almost invariably be chopped back with a spade, and problems only arise when they become entwined with other plants that are less vigorous.

BELOW   *Hosta and astilbe provide an ideal, shade-tolerant ground cover with minimal maintenance.*

BOTTOM   *The soft carpet of plants, juxtaposed with the granite paving and terracotta column, makes the perfect combination of hard and soft landscape.*

OPPOSITE   *Ground cover can be planted formally in regular clumps, or informally as shown here. This treatment is delightful for its use of the bench and uses a wide range of plants, including perennial geranium, alchemilla, pulmonaria and box.*

Sunny planting

ABOVE *It is essential to soften a dramatic change of level with planting. In a sunny situation the choice is very wide, and here climbers have been well used to link the areas together.*

OPPOSITE *Actinidia kolomikta needs sun to produce those wonderful coloured leaves. It will thrive on a sunny wall, provided there is an adequate depth of soil and irrigation is available.*

The vast majority of plants, like people, enjoy sunny conditions. If you plan a garden, it makes sense that the main planted areas should if possible be in a sunny or open position. Some plants, however, are particularly specialized and tolerate the extremes of a hot, arid climate or situation. Many of these come from warm or sub-tropical countries and therefore some are not altogether hardy when planted in the colder latitudes.

Many sun-loving plants have grey foliage: in fact, grey-leaved plants almost invariably need sun to really thrive. Their leaves either have a covering of down or a waxy texture as a direct defence against the sun's rays: this reduces the amount of water the plant loses and subsequently needs to take up. Good

examples are *Senecio greyi*, *Stachys byzantina*, the glaucous-leaved hebes, rosemary, lavender, and santolina. Of course, not all sun-lovers are grey-leaved. Other excellent choices would include evergreens such as cistus, ceanothus, escallonia and the sword-like leaves of yucca and phormium.

Where cold weather and the frosts of winter can be a problem, it is worth remembering that the majority of hardy or half-hardy annuals will not survive outdoors throughout the year. Virtually all of these enjoy full sun and are invaluable as fillers or as a source of instant colour in both borders and containers. Use annuals in bold drifts, respecting the colour scheme of neighbouring shrubs and herbaceous plants.

Shady planting

In nature certain species of plants have adapted to thrive in quite specific conditions. The difference between sun and shade or light and shadow can mean a great deal in botanic terms and this same selectivity is reflected in the ever-increasing range of plants grown for the garden.

Most species thrive in an open, sunny position, but those that do equally well in the shade are rather more limited. Town gardens are frequently small and surrounded by high walls, which means that much of the area could be in shade for most of the day. In a courtyard or basement, the light levels could be very low indeed.

Many of the best shade-loving shrubs are tough evergreens, which often have the benefit of flower and berry. Favourites in this category include skimmia, fatsia, arundinaria, mahonia, aucuba, prunus laurocerasus, sarcococca, and euonymus. Watch for plants with variegated leaves which tend to reflect light and lighten the composition gener-

ally in a dark situation. Such plants can give the garden a three-dimensional structure into which more delicate herbaceous plants can be woven.

When selecting from the ample choice of shade-loving herbaceous plants, remember that dramatic foliage can be as important as flower. Hosta is an absolute must, either for damp beds or for containers, while Japanese anemone, helleborus, aquilegia, digitalis, bergenia and dicentra are also an excellent choice for shade.

Climbing plants or shrubs which can be trained against a wall are vital in a small, dark, walled area, and there is more choice than you might at first think. All the ivies are excellent, with their wide range of plain and variegated evergreen foliage. Pyracantha bears masses of berries and also holds its leaves throughout the winter. For flower, clematis is indispensable, along with the climbing *Hydrangea anomala* subsp. *petiolaris* and the winter-flowering *Jasminum nudiflorum*.

ABOVE *Hostas, polygonatum and Philadelphus coronarius 'Variegatus' stand out beautifully.*

LEFT *Both shrubs and annuals have been used here and their juxtaposition does much to soften the steps.*

OPPOSITE *With some careful planting, trees can provide a screen of privacy but still admit quantities of beautiful dappled sunlight.*

Hardy perennials

Where shrubs are the backbone of the garden, hardy perennials are the fillers that bring delicacy and colour into the overall theme. By definition, they can withstand a wide range of temperatures and most, although not all, die down in winter and reappear the following spring. There is a hardy perennial for every soil and situation from full sun to deep shade, from bone-dry to permanently wet bog. If you choose correctly, you can have flowers throughout the year and the foliage of many is outstanding. Some, such as acanthus, aruncus or ligularia, can stand by themselves as focal points, although most look best in a drift or group. Such drifts can weave a pattern, leading the eye around a corner or linking together other types of plant material. Make sure to respect the underlying colour scheme of the garden. Remember that a carefully graded border does much to increase the visual size of even a small plot. Size, too, is

immensely variable, from the inspiring white panicles of *Crambe cordifolia*, a full 1.8m (6ft) high, to the tiny leaves and flowers of viola, barely off the ground. Plants such as hosta are also invaluable not only for their range of broad handsome leaves, but also because they tolerate both sun and shade, making excellent ground cover beneath taller plants.

The fact that many such plants die down in winter does not mean they fail as weed suppressors — weeds will not germinate at this time of the year and by the time the new growth starts most hardy perennials have formed sufficient leaf to shade out any competition.

One important point to bear in mind is the fact that many varieties enjoy ample watering, particularly in the heat of summer. Regular irrigation at this time will be rewarded by handsome foliage and a wealth of flower. Another advantage of these versatile plants is their speed of growth. In my own

OPPOSITE *Pink roses and white phlox ensure the unity of this lovely, raggle-taggle border, their colours harmonizing beautifully, and the dense planting means that virtually all weeds have been eliminated.*

RIGHT *Dianthus, geranium, digitalis and cistus provide the colour harmony, while raised beds boost smaller species and simplify maintenance.*

BELOW *Pulsatilla and muscari are excellent planting partners. Both are spring flowering and both enjoy an open, sunny position.*

garden they were the first thing I planted and within eighteen months they had filled out the borders in a subtle blend of flower and foliage. This approach can give you a breathing space in which to develop the overall planting design of a garden and sections of herbaceous plants can then be removed to allow the introduction of shrubs which will also act as a partial support to some of the taller perennials. It is a misconception that shrubs can support everything, however, and it is well worth using simple metal frames that are completely unobtrusive once the plants develop. If you are going to stake, do it early in the season. Hardy perennials are also comparatively cheap; when you consider that they can be divided up to form several new plants after a few years, discarding the older, less vigorous sections of root, they really are excellent value. They are also easily moved – autumn and early spring being the best seasons. Spring is also the ideal time

for forking in a well-rotted organic fertilizer. During the rapid summer growing season a liquid fertilizer will keep things in peak condition.

Some hardy perennials are evergreen and these can be invaluable. Some of my own favourites are within the vast family of euphorbias. *Euphorbia wulfenii*, with its handsome architectural stems, is one of the most impressive. Another good choice is *Euphorbia amygdaloides* var. *robbiae* which is a useful ground cover in shade; it grows to a maximum of .6m (2ft) and has dark green rosettes on erect stems. A plant that no garden should be without is *Euphorbia amygdaloides* 'Rubra', with stunning purple foliage that adds colour in winter. In spring it has the most attractive and unusual bracts. A final choice that is a must for all dark corners so common in town gardens is *Helleborus corsicus*, with evergreen sculptural leaves and unusual green flowers that are borne in February.

Containers

Pots and containers of every kind are a vital element of a town garden. Not only are they a vehicle for plant material but they can act as ornaments and focal points in their own right. If used for the latter purpose, they need not necessarily even contain plants at all; if this is the case the shape of the pot is obviously important. More often than not, however, pots will be host to plant material and the position of the containers within the garden will obviously influence the choice of shrubs, hardy perennials or annual material.

The correct method of filling containers is covered elsewhere in the book, but as a general rule the bigger the pot the happier plants will be, drying out less quickly and having a more generous root run. In the final analysis, providing feeding and watering are done on a regular basis, the pot will determine the eventual size of the occupant, simply by restricting the development of the roots.

A common and effective way of dealing with pots is to plant bulbs for colour early in the year and follow this with a selection of half-hardy annuals that take one through the summer until the first frosts. Hanging baskets and window boxes can be treated in exactly the same way, while a trough or small raised bed can be the ideal situation for a collection of alpine plants. To give colour and interest over a longer period, shrubs are the answer and here there is virtually no limitation to what you can grow. Obviously, very large and vigorous species would be impractical but most varieties that are suitable for a small town garden, including climbers, will be fine. Some shrubs positively thrive: camellias, hydrangeas, skimmias, dwarf rhododendron and Japanese acers are good examples. Heathers and miniature conifers can also be grown in containers and fruit trees grown on dwarfing root-stock will also be satisfactory.

ABOVE RIGHT *One of the most useful functions of pots is the ability to move them around, not only within a garden but between the house and your outside room.*

RIGHT *When planted properly the container itself becomes incidental. Here daisies, ivy-leaved pelargoniums and hosta provide a perfect mix.*

OPPOSITE *A sense of humour is vital in the garden. Look at the terracotta cushions and how the variegated ivy mimics the spirally clipped box bush.*

something special for you from a previously prepared drawing. Fix the arrangement, which can mimic statuary of any kind as well as birds and animals, firmly into the ground, and plant a number of the smaller-leaved ivies round the base or close by. The result will be spectacular and virtually maintenance-free as the plants will run up and over the surface, keeping to but softening the outline in the process. One of the best varieties would be *Hedera helix* 'Gold Heart' or *Hedera helix* 'Glacier'. Both of these are tolerant of shade and, with their handsome variegated foliage, will stand out well in a darkened area.

A slight variation on this technique is to create a hybrid between a fence and a hedge. The principle is exactly the same, with plants scrambling over a metal or plastic mesh. Depending on the strength of the climber, such a construction can be quite high and make an excellent internal divider or screen within the garden. It will not need regular cutting, an occasional trim or selective thinning being all that is really necessary.

As well as true climbers, there are a number of shrubs that make a very good job of leaning against a wall and, in fact, do the better for it. If you are lucky enough to have a sunny courtyard, the opportunities are endless, and, bearing in mind the slightly higher annual temperatures in town, you can take a slight risk and grow one or two relatively tender plants. Of these one of the finest is ceanothus, a shrub of some size with mainly evergreen foliage and superb blue flowers. Another excellent choice for a high wall would be *Cytisus battandieri*, a member of the broom family, but with foliage similar to laburnum. It is a glorious plant, bearing cone-shaped clusters of flowers that smell of pineapple. It is not a plant for a tiny garden, but if you have the space it is more than worthwhile. One of the most valuable flowering shrubs to enjoy the backing of a wall is *Chaenomeles speciosa*. This is available in many varieties, ranging from white through pink to red. They are adaptable to shade and have quince-like fruit later in the year.

Berry is as important as flower, and there are many useful wall shrubs to provide it. Perhaps one of the best known is *Cotoneaster horizontalis*. This is excellent for a north or east wall, having a profusion of berries and autumn-coloured foliage. A final choice is pyracantha, an evergreen with yellow or orange berries borne in huge clusters.

OPPOSITE *Pergolas and arches are perfect for climbing plants, providing ample room to grow away from the restrictions of walls and the overhanging eaves of a house. The structure is often immaterial once it is covered with foliage: here rustic poles are smothered with wisteria. One should bear in mind, however, the durability of these structures. Poles, such as the simple ones used here, although cheap and easy to erect, are susceptible to rot and a more permanent structure would use either pressure-treated softwood or a hardwood.*

BELOW *Vines are indispensible climbers, clinging with tendrils and having foliage that often provides glorious autumn colour. Two of the most attractive are Vitis coignetiae, with leaves 25cm (10in) long and 20cm (8in) wide, and another possible choice, Vitis vinifera, which in early summer has reddish brown leaves, then turning to purple in the autumn. An added bonus of this vine is its edible fruits.*

Shrubs and conifers

Shrubs are the backbone of any garden, providing screening, shelter, the exclusion of bad views and of course interest in their own right. We have already seen that large, mainly evergreen species provide the framework and support for the lighter, more delicate material to follow. Not all shrubs are bulky: many are small ground-hugging varieties that can either form a point of emphasis or act as an ideal low-maintenance carpet.

Of course the secret to good planting design is to produce a mix of material that will provide colour and interest throughout the year. A garden full of shrubs would almost inevitably be a little heavy in visual terms and it needs the addition of hardy perennials and annuals to lift the composition and bring it to life.

Many shrubs are evergreen and many have variegated foliage. It is always worth remembering that flowers will only last a relatively short time, so a

ABOVE *This delicious white hydrangea stands out because it was planted in front of the dark, glossy leaves of laurel. The round, clipped box with its tiny leaves also provides an interesting contrast in texture, the whole group forming a well-studied exercise in planting design.*

OPPOSITE *Scale is important in any garden but at the front of a house vertical emphasis can help to balance the mass of a building. Pyracantha and holly can both be used to good advantage, having evergreen foliage and the benefit of winter berries. Berries have the added benefit of attracting birds, always a welcome sight in town.*

variety of textures or attractive foliage is of paramount importance. A garden should, after all, look good for twelve months of the year and not just provide a flush of interest at one given time.

Conifers are not shrubs in the true sense of the word, but the way in which they are used certainly affects the overall composition. In many ways they are the punctuation marks of a garden, their strong, often columnar outline drawing the eye. Bearing this in mind, they should be used sparingly as focal points. Virtually all are evergreen and the very large and fast-growing types, although often suggested for screening purposes, are really too vigorous for anything but the largest garden.

If you are really keen on these delightful plants, a collection of miniature varieties can be quite superb and this is the best way to see the contrasts in height, shape and foliage to the best advantage. Many prostrate conifers form excellent ground cover and can be used in conjunction with heathers to form an ever-changing carpet throughout the year. It is quite possible to create a small garden completely planted with conifers and, although this is a somewhat purist approach, it can reduce maintenance to a very low level indeed. Many of the junipers are prostrate in habit, and, while some are too large for a small garden, varieties such as *Juniperus squamata* 'Blue Star', *Juniperus horizontalis* 'Glauca' and *Juniperus × media* 'Gold Coast' are an excellent choice. Team these with more upright types which might include *Picea pungens* 'Koster' or *Thuja plicata* 'Rogersii' and you will set up a fascinating dialogue. Although most conifers are evergreen, there is an unusual miniature larch, *Larix kaempferi* 'Nana', that is certainly worth growing. This will lose its needles during the winter but the compact, tightly grouped branches have a sculptural pattern of their own.

Many conifers are suitable for planting in containers; so, too, are a good range of shrubs. The advantages of growing shrubs in containers in a small urban plot have already been outlined, but you need to select material that is not too rampant.

One real bonus of shrubs in containers is the fact that you can alter the acidity of the soil and grow shrubs like azalea and rhododendron that would perish in the open border. Many of the smaller varieties are ideal, and the recently developed *Rhododendron yakushimanum* hybrids are perfect for containers. Apart from a wealth of bloom, they have subtle colouring on the undersides of their leaves.

The Japanese evergreen azaleas are another good choice; even when the blossom is over the glossy foliage looks excellent throughout the year.

Larger acid-loving shrubs that do particularly well in pots are the camellias. These, too, are evergreen with spring blossom that marks the end of winter. In town they can appear very early in the year and, as the blooms can be damaged by morning sun after frost, they are best positioned in a north- or west-facing site where they will be at their best. People frequently rearrange furniture in a room, but rarely do the same thing with plants in the garden. As long as you remember what plant enjoys a particular situation, the end result will be fascinating. You can quickly and easily change the whole character of your outside room. The only drawback of large shrubs in large pots is the regular job of feeding and irrigating, although there is now plenty of equipment to make life a lot easier. Large shrubs planted in large containers will obviously be virtually impossible to move about, so fit them with a set of heavy-duty castors.

As a final link between inside and out remember that many shrubs are ideal for cutting, the stems being used for floral arrangements. In spring the catkins of hazel and the smaller willows are delightful, while later in the year the glorious purple leaves and flowers of *Cotinus coggygria* 'Foliis Purpureis' or the silver of *Pyrus salicifolia* 'Pendula' contribute to any interior decoration.

ABOVE LEFT *Evergreen Japanese azaleas form an unusual and attractive low hedge that will be full of blossom during the spring. This planting is also evergreen which provides interest throughout the year and makes an interesting alternative to box.*

LEFT *Conifers, with their strong sculptural outline, are the punctuation marks of a garden. In this architectural setting they look just right, echoing the soaring buildings in the background.*

OPPOSITE *Foliage is so often more important than flower, providing interest over a far longer period – it also adds texture to a garden. All these plants are suitable for a shady wall and include bergenia, astilbe, hydrangea and rodgersia.*

Trees

Trees in a town garden can be a real hazard. So often you will see a garden that is completely dominated by a tree which is far too large, often with the accompanying problems of leaf fall, dense shade and, in some cases, structural damage by an invasive root system. Should you inherit this kind of situation, and it is not uncommon, there may well be a real need to selectively thin the canopy or reduce the height of the crown. Remember, though,

that many city trees are protected and permission may well have to be sought if you wish to remove one altogether from your garden.

In a natural landscape or environment trees form the highest level of vegetation, something that is naturally echoed in the garden. Here, of course, we are not always looking for a dense cover of foliage, although a well-sited specimen can do much to block the view from adjoining windows. One of the

main roles of a tree in garden planning terms is to act as a point of emphasis.

In a small garden there will only be room for one or perhaps two trees and their choice will need to take into account their eventual size, shape and general appearance. This eliminates virtually all the 'forest' trees such as oak, chestnut, sycamore, beech and the larger willows. Primarily, you need to look at smaller species, amongst which the following might be ideal.

Many of the birch (betula) make an ideal choice for a town garden. Although they are deciduous, the bark of specimens more than ten years old is extremely striking in winter. The foliage is light and delicate, filtering the sun rather than blocking it out altogether. A particularly fine variety is *Betula utilis* subsp. *jacquemontii*, while the smaller *Betula pendula* 'Youngii', the weeping birch, is ideal in a small plot.

Most varieties of the malus (flowering crab apple) are fine, with the bonus of blossom and fruit, while many flowering cherries (prunus) are also ideal, with their early spring blossom. Be careful of the colour, though, as the more vibrant pinks look uncomfortable against other spring foliage.

Sorbus, too, is a good choice, with the benefit of autumn berry, while *Robinia pseudoacacia* 'Frisia' has glorious golden foliage. Many varieties of acer have fine bark and foliage and, for an evergreen that can either be grown as a tree or cut back hard each year to form a vigorous shrub, try *Eucalyptus gunnii*.

Although trees are large, they are only plants. It is a sad fact that most people not only forget to feed them regularly but also give them little support in the first vital years while their root system is getting established. Always prepare a good pit and mix fertilizer and peat with the soil to give an ideal growing medium. Drive in the stake before planting the tree, as doing it afterwards can so easily sever a root.

Imagination is the key to a good garden. Why not use trees to form an arch or alley? Several varieties, including lime and hornbeam, are ideal for this. The technique is known as pleaching and entails growing the trees over wires or frames until they meet. The foliage and branches can then be pruned into shape, creating a combination of sculpture and garden architecture. A living pergola may involve a little more maintenance than a straightforward timber one, but the end result can be much more exciting and satisfying in the long run.

OPPOSITE *Trees can soften a town garden and screen a bad or overlooked aspect. Conifers, although evergreen, are not always a good choice as the stronger growing species quickly outstrip their allocated space. This garden has been wrapped about with deciduous species and shrubs at a lower level reduce maintenance to a minimum.*

ABOVE *On a roof planting is important to soften the line of surrounding buildings. This composition is pure roofscape and is complemented by the surrounding trees that frame the pretty cupola. Robinia pseudoacacia 'Frisia' with its yellow foliage, is a particularly dramatic choice.*

Herbs and vegetables

The heyday of the true vegetable garden, particularly in the confines of the smaller town garden, has now largely disappeared. There has recently, however, been an increasing awareness of the advantages of crops grown at home that can be harvested without the concern that they may have been subject to inorganic fertilizers and chemical pesticides. It is also true that many vegetables and practically all herbs are particularly good-looking in their own right and so have a double role to play in the overall development of the garden.

The method in which they are planted depends to a certain extent on their habit and eventual size. Many vegetables can be mixed into the borders – a technique often used to good advantage on the Continent. Such plants as globe artichokes, sweet corn, savoy cabbage, marrows and pumpkins all have a handsome, architectural shape. Add to this the glorious flower and foliage of runner beans and the advantages of 'mixed' gardening are immediately apparent. The salad crops, including lettuce, carrots, radishes, spring onions and tomatoes, are also ideal in a small area. Of course not all vegetables need to be grown in open ground; pots and containers are fine, and the latest trend of

'growing bags', although not visually attractive, certainly has advantages in terms of intensive production, particularly in the confines of a tiny balcony. Herbs, on the other hand, are absolutely ideal grown in containers, or in a self-contained raised bed, as these help to restrict an often vigorous root run. Some of the larger types, such as angelica and fennel, are too big for pots, but look superb with other types of planting in the borders.

Fruit should also be included in this section and here again foliage can play an important role. Rhubarb, for instance, is a very handsome garden plant, as well as an effective ground cover. Strawberries are ideal grown in pots but do remember to net against birds. Many bushes bearing berries are attractive – redcurrants, blackcurrants, loganberries and blackberries are well worth inclusion and can be neatly trained into a relatively small space. So too can fruit trees, particularly if grown as espaliers or cordons along wires or against a wall. (Always make sure to choose the correct shape of fruits to suit the size and shape of your garden.) As a final masterpiece try growing a fig. This will be happiest against a sunny wall, and has superb foliage with delicious fruit for you to enjoy.

LOW-MAINTENANCE PLANTING

OPPOSITE *Herbs are both handsome and practical, with the bonus of aromatic leaves. Here they are laid out in a traditional pattern with low box hedges defining the beds. The best variety for such hedges is Buxus sempervirens 'Suffruticosa' which produces neat tight growth but for a rather faster alternative you could try Lonicera nitida.*

ABOVE *To grow vegetables on a roof is already fulfilling but to enjoy such a view as this is sheer magic. Salad crops thrive in these hot, sunny conditions provided there is ample irrigation. Obviously the more vigorous root vegetables are impractical although with growing bags even these are possible. A good depth of soil is important as will be regular feeding and irrigation.*

DESIGN SOLUTIONS

To create a design and subsequently build a garden is a rewarding achievement. It involves carrying out a basic survey of the plot, analyzing what you need, choosing materials and, of course, selecting plants. It follows, therefore, that by producing a design, or a number of designs, you eliminate mistakes and make the final job of construction as foolproof as possible. Always remember that it is difficult to incorporate a feature once the composition is finalized. A good design that revolves around a sensible combination of hard and soft landscape features, tailored to your particular requirements, will also reduce maintenance to a minimum. Remember that no two gardens are ever alike – one reason the subject is so fascinating.

In an urban situation there are many more dissimilar plots than there are in the suburbs. The shapes of buildings, the layouts of streets and the direction of railway lines or rivers make sure of that. Although the design sequence for any garden remains constant, the way in which the composition develops and eventually crystallizes will be as diverse as the city itself. Some town gardens are rectangular, others have a dog-leg, some are in the shape of a triangle, some are in basements or courtyards, others on balconies and roofs.

Because many town gardens are small, as we have seen, they can be thought of as outside rooms. However, while many of us are happy to plan the spaces inside the house, once we move

ABOVE *A pierced brick wall has a mellow feel and is further softened here by the planting.*

OPPOSITE *All the ingredients of a successful town garden are displayed here with considerable panache. This garden, designed by Tim Du Val, provides a well-handled change of level, contrasting surfaces, raised beds and a feeling of space and movement softened by planting.*

outside the problems seem altogether more difficult. There is no real reason why this should be so, but it is all too often the case. It seems easy enough to choose a sensible floor covering or carpet, but many people's choice of paving is a near disaster. No one would think of planning a room with corners or angles that made using a vacuum cleaner impossible, but many lawns do just that for a mower. Even when furniture inside the home is well designed and practical, the room outside may have a flimsy set of bent-wire chairs that look awful and feel even more uncomfortable. In short, the common perception of a garden is far from practical and that is precisely why so many plots end up as never-ending burdens.

In this chapter different design solutions for gardens of broadly similar characteristics will be considered. All of them have been chosen because of their ability to overcome a certain problem and for their inherent interest and obvious success as outside rooms. At the end of each section, I explain my own ideas. They are based on experience of preparing schemes for similar plots in cities all over the world.

If there is one single criteria that brings success to a garden, it is simplicity. Unfortunately, to many people this is an elusive ingredient even though it produces a pattern that is easy on the eye and low on maintenance. Remember, too, that by copying something you lose the spontaneity that made it attractive in the first place.

Front Garden

ABOVE This front garden has a perfect balance between hard and soft landscape. Pots have been used to extend the line of beds while the white overhead beams link the sides of the composition. The harder lines of the building are softened with climbing plants. Remember that this area can also be attractive for sitting, so the seat in this garden is an ideal addition.

OPPOSITE ABOVE Here a composition of paving, planting and water is at an angle to the main path, setting up an interesting pattern which brings this small front garden alive. Planting includes pulmonaria, hosta and vinca, while the pool has been well stocked with aquatic plants. Sensible brick coping has been used around both the pool and raised bed to minimize frost damage.

It is a great pity that front gardens are so often ignored. It is quite true that in many instances the distance between house and street is minimal, but this makes it even more important that the space be handled with a degree of sensitivity. While a back garden is primarily for leisure, the area at the front of the house revolves around access, both for people and vehicles. The pace of life here is quicker and this will have to be reflected in the design.

There may well be ample room for parking, although the way in which parking areas relate to the rest of the composition is sometimes dubious. Often drives and parking areas are the largest single elements within the garden. In order to provide continuity, you should use materials which blend in with the house. What you should not do is compromise by leaving part of an old scheme in place and 'tacking on' new conflicting materials. Matching new and old is always difficult and the design will more often than not look, uncomfortable. Neither is this particularly cost-effective, as the original surface will almost certainly need replacement sooner or later.

As hard landscape may predominate in the front garden, the provision and selection of planting will balance the composition. If pollution is a problem, there are many trees and shrubs that are particularly resistant. Much city air is, however, becoming increasingly cleaner and usually a wide selection of plants can be grown easily. The best ideas may be found from a walk around the neighbourhood to see just what does do well.

It is also true that plants have different characters: while softly planted borders may engender a feeling of relaxation in the rear garden, their opposites may be more appropriate in the front. Here one might think of using the architectural lines of yucca, acanthus, phormium or mahonia. A background of tougher plants will not only improve noise problems, but may also discourage short-cuts by the postman or delivery man. So, too, will a well-placed boulder on the corner of a bed – far better than a squashed plant and good-looking into the bargain. Pots and window boxes can provide instant colour. Try to blend functional necessities into the overall scheme – a well-concealed and neatly constructed binstore or a cleverly disguised oil tank smothered in climbing plants will fit happily into the pattern. As a final point, remember that first impressions count, and make the best out of this front approach.

There is no doubt that many front gardens are a genuinely awkward shape. This is a typical example, being complicated by the fact that the front door is roughly in the middle of the property while the drive is far to the side. There are various criteria that need fulfilling here — the main one being access for both car and people. At the same time the garden needs to look attractive and maintenance should be kept to a minimum.

As the width is considerable, it was decided to have two main routes to the front door — one straight off the street, the other passing along the front of the building from the drive. In order to provide continuity, two paving materials were chosen, brick being teamed with a precast concrete slab. These interlock with the raised bed to form an interesting pattern that leads both feet and eye through the space. The dominant drive was played down by carrying the line of the brick path across the

BELOW *Where a house has a balanced elevation, the garden can follow suit with a formal design. Here brick paving has been teamed with crisp precast concrete slabs to frame the beds and make a straight path to the gate. Planting is confined largely to annuals. A firmer structure of shrubs would provide greater winter interest.*

parking area. The bricks were also laid in a stretcher bond that displays a strong directional emphasis, leading towards the main entrance. Archways, which are hosts for climbers, straddle the paths, while two beds for ivy provide evergreen colour and minimal maintenance. Grass was considered impractical, and instead a combination of cobbles, boulders and ground cover occupy an area to the left of the front door, providing a slightly Japanese look and again requiring little work.

FRONT GARDEN PLANT LIST

1 *Chamaecyparis lawsoniana* 'Minima Aurea'
2 *Ballota pseudictamnus*
3 *Cistus* 'Silver Pink'
4 *Kniphofia* 'Royal Standard'
5 *Euphorbia wulfenii*
6 *Mahonia* 'Charity'
7 *Skimmia × foremanii*
8 *Pulmonaria saccharata*
9 *Daphne mezereum*
10 *Arundinaria nitida*
11 *Hosta sieboldiana*
12 *Aucuba japonica* 'Crotonifolia'
13 *Epimedium grandiflorum*
14 *Spiraea × arguta*
15 *Kerria japonica*
16 *Hypericum* 'Hidcote'
17 *Hydrangea paniculata* 'Grandiflora'
18 *Cedrus deodara* 'Golden Horizon'
19 *Erica herbacea* 'Myretoun Ruby'
20 *Picea glauca var. albertiana* 'Conica'
21 *Erica herbacea* 'Springwood White'
22 *Hedera colchica* 'Dentata Variegata'
23 *Hosta sieboldiana*
24 *Hydrangea macrophylla* 'Blue Wave'
25 *Berberis thunbergii* 'Atropurpurea Nana'
26 *Choisya ternata*
27 *Betula utilis subsp. jaquemontii* (ALONG FRONT)
28 *Hebe* 'Midsummer Beauty'
29 *Lavandula vera*
30 *Euonymus japonicus* 'Ovatus Aureus'
31 *Ruta* 'Jackmans Blue'
32 *Rosmarinus* 'Miss Jessop's variety'
33 *Festuca glauca*
34 *Wisteria sinensis*
35 *Hebe rakaiensis*
36 *Cistus × lusitanicus* 'Decumbens'
37 *Picea glauca var. albertina* 'Conica'
38 *Berberis thunbergii* 'Atropurpurea Nana'
39 *Festuca glauca*
40 *Avena candida*
41 *Ophiopogon planiscapus* 'Nigrescens'
42 *Hedera helix* 'Gold Heart'
43 *Hedera helix* 'Glacier'
44 *Elaeagnus × ebbingii*
45 *Iris pallida* 'Argenteo Variegata'
46 *Salvia officinalis* 'Tricolor'

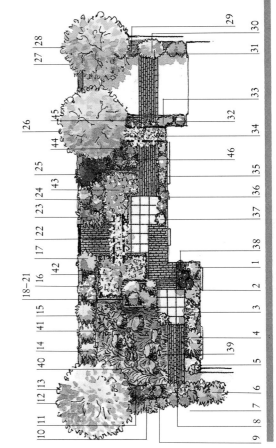

Basements and Courtyards

If there are two types of garden that are synonymous with the city, they are the basement and the courtyard. With so many walls and the jostle of buildings there are a multitude of spaces left over that are eagerly snapped up as a haven for both plants and people. The common denominator is, of course, the fact that they are surrounded on all sides – a fact providing both advantages and disadvantages.

Courtyards

Courtyards are usually larger than basements but both have the great asset of shelter. Most courtyards are protected from the worst of wind and weather, which means that, provided there is at least a degree of sunshine throughout the day, the space will become an ideal outdoor room. City gardens usually have a milder climate than their suburban or rural counterparts, and this increases the range of plant materials that can be used.

Because of surrounding walls or fences, which are more often than not of a considerable height, the entire courtyard composition can be treated in an essentially architectural manner. In this way you can create a strong bond between inside and out in a number of ways. One of the most obvious will be to link materials, either with brick paving matching that used in the building or with a floor material that starts within the house and continues into the garden. This transition could be made a good deal easier with room-height sliding glass doors, reinforced by planting on both sides of the divide. It is worth remembering that many house plants can also live outside if they are 'hardened off'. These include *Fatsia japonica*, fatshedera and ivies of virtually every description. This makes the dividing line between house and garden less distinct.

Colour can also be used to good advantage, with a scheme from a room inside being continued on a garden wall. Remember to respect the height of the ceiling so that the transition between the two elements is as visually smooth as possible.

High walls surrounding a courtyard can create a different set of problems. Privacy may be threatened if the space is overlooked by neighbouring windows. Overhead beams can break those unwanted sight-lines and also act as hosts for fragrant climbing plants. Another trick to reduce a feeling of

claustrophobia is again to use overhead beams and to match the height of these to a colour scheme that is run around the height of the courtyard walls. The beams would not surround the entire space but the line of the paint scheme would create a 'false ceiling'. If white or cream is used, as much available light as possible will be reflected and the problem of dark surrounding buildings can be overcome. Pale colours used on the ground will also reflect light. There are a number of precast concrete slabs that are light grey or almost white and small stone chippings in a similar colour not only reflect light but provide an interesting change in texture. Use such a surface in conjunction with architectural planting and the result is dramatic, the leaves and paving sharply contrasting with one another.

Another way of introducing light and an illusion of space is by using mirrors. The fashion of *trompe-l'œil*, or false perspective, is heavily overplayed in many town gardens, rarely being anything but much too obvious. Mirrors can, however, be used to great effect if well sited and subtly integrated into a planted area.

Courtyards are also the ideal vehicle for raised beds, giving plants a much needed boost to soften surrounding walls. Such beds also do much to reduce maintenance, as tending plants from a standing or sitting position is a good deal easier than working at ground level. The ideally planted bed is bursting with foliage, plants trailing over the edges as well as climbing on the surrounding walls.

While planting and paving appeal largely in visual terms, sound and scent are equally important. A courtyard with surrounding walls can do much to reduce external noise to a whisper and can provide shelter which allows scented plants to come into their own. Many of the latter are particularly tolerant of the shady conditions so frequently found in this sort of situation; they include *Choisya ternata*, philadelphus, sarcococca, skimmia, ligustrum and that invaluable annual *Nicotiana*.

Noise is a scourge in the city and, to escape it, even for a while, is time well spent. In a garden laden with scent the appeal of moving water and its associated noise can be irresistible. No need here for a roaring waterfall or pompous fountain – rather the gentle plash of a bubble jet within an almost still pool or perhaps water gently sliding from a raised pool to another at a lower level. These are enough to create an invaluable atmosphere of tranquillity.

ABOVE This long narrow courtyard sets a linear pattern that is reflected in the garden design. Paths, planting and water are set in parallel lines that echo the surrounding boundaries and focus on the position of doors and windows, capitalizing on the linear nature of the space rather than trying to work against it.

Planting is largely evergreen and reduces maintenance to a very low level. It is interesting that when a garden is viewed from above the linear pattern of the plan is far more evident. This can be useful in the layout stage when the design can be pegged out with string. By doing this you can see how the shapes relate to one another and it will be easy enough to make any adjustments or try out alternatives before starting on construction.

Basements

It is a pity that so many basement gardens fail to realize their true potential. They do, of course, have limitations, usually being small and shady. Their function is largely one of access, perhaps leading to a basement apartment. In this respect they have much in common with a front garden.

Steps leading down to a basement must be as safe as possible. In some instances, the old steps may be quite inadequate and it can make sense to re-plan the flight, taking up rather more space than they previously occupied. The floor of the area can be tiny, little more than a landing between the bottom of the steps and the door. Even so, there is scope here to create a worthwhile composition of the kind shown opposite. Here paving is a combination of a very pale precast concrete slab and brick, the former reflecting as much light as possible. The brick highlights the front door as well as creating a frame for the slabs.

As there may be a considerable change in level between the street and the basement floor, planting will be a great asset to temper high walls. Raised beds, here as in the courtyard, can be particularly valuable, bridging that gap with flower and foliage. If such beds adjoin the house, remember that you must provide a vertical damp-proof course to prevent damp-associated problems inside. In this design the beds have been kept to either end of the basement, those adjoining the steps being set at different levels to provide greater interest. Space for dustbins or gas and electricity meters can be a

ABOVE *In such a tiny backyard it is extremely difficult to provide interest. Here that has been created admirably as well as room to sit and dine. Trellis has been used to subdivide the space and a well placed mirror increases the visual dimension*

enormously, without being too obvious. The neatly tiled floor creates an interesting pattern that is echoed in the trellis and glazing bars of adjoining doors and windows. (Garden designed by Christopher Masson.)

STEPS   49, 118, 125

SHADY PLANTING   60, 138–41

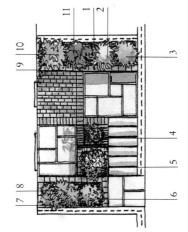

problem. Here they have been neatly fitted beneath the raised bed, out of sight and accessible by a hinged door.

Because of the deep shade, selection of suitable plants will be vital. Here a largely evergreen range that will provide colour and interest throughout the year is used. Climbers, too, will be important and this is where the family of ivies comes into its own, many having the bonus of brightly variegated foliage and all having the essential benefit of being tolerant of deep shade.

TINY BASEMENT GARDEN
PLANT LIST
1 Hedera helix 'Glacier'
2 Hosta fortunei 'Albopicta'
3 Sarcococca humilis
4 Arundinaria viridistriata (IN TUB)
5 Hydrangea macrophylla 'Nikko Blue'
6 Aucuba japonica 'Crotonifolia'
7 × Fatshedera lizei
8 Polystichum setiferum 'Divisilobum'
9 Hedera helix 'Gold Heart'
10 Fatsia japonica
11 Helleborus corsicus

Courtyards

My own courtyard design is set within a typical walled garden and embraces all the best elements this type of composition has to offer.

Moving away from the building, there is a sensible paved area that uses square precast concrete slabs in a pale colour. To keep maintenance to an absolute minimum, the remaining floor is covered with gravel laid over a weak mix of concrete that eliminates weed growth. Architectural plants have been allowed to grow through this surface in selected areas, while pots act as hosts for both annuals and herbs. Raised beds interlock with one another at different heights. The water feature is split into three levels, one pool falling into another with just a whisper of sound.

The planting is particularly important and caters for the swing of the sun throughout the day. Certain areas are in almost permanent shade while others enjoy the sunny, sheltered conditions that only a courtyard can provide.

ABOVE LEFT *Brick paving provides a small-scale intimate surface — ideal for the difficult cutting-in around the central pool and fountain. The sitting area is positioned to catch the sun, and planting is well chosen to soften the walls.*

LEFT *Generous steps lead up to this tiny courtyard which has been filled to the brim with luscious planting. The two pots at the top of the steps focus the view towards the centrally placed urn which in turn leads the eye up to the wall.*

COURTYARD GARDEN
PLANT LIST

1 *Betula pendula* 'Youngii'
2 *Ceanothus thyrsiflorus* var. *repens*
3 *Acer palmatum* 'Dissectum
   Atropurpureum'
4 *Scirpus lacustris* subsp. *tabernaemontani*
   'Zebrinus'
5 *Eucalpytus gunnii*
6 *Clematis montana* 'Tetrarose'
7 *Choisya ternata*
8 *Verbascum bombyciferum*
9 *Ligularia stenocephala* 'The Rocket'
10 *Rheum palmatum* 'Bowles variety'
11 *Actinidia chinensis*
12 *Phormium tenax* 'Variegatum'
13 *Ceanothus* 'Delight'
14 *Sedum* 'Autumn Joy'
15 *Geranium* 'Johnson's Blue'
16 Zonal pelargoniums (IN POT)
17 *Hedera helix* 'Glacier'
18 *Jasminum officinale*
19 *Typha minima*
20 Herbs in pots
21 *Thymus × citriodorus* 'Aureus'
22 *Artemisia arborescens*
23 *Vitis vinifera* 'Purpurea'
24 *Salvia officinalis* 'Purpurascens'
25 *Epimedium × rubrum*
26 *Hydrangea macrophylla* 'Blue Wave'
27 *Bergenia* 'Silberlicht'
28 *Euonymus fortunei* 'Silver Queen'
29 *Ajuga reptans* 'Burgundy Glow'

30 *Arundinaria viridistriata*
31 *Hydrangea anomala* subsp. *petiolaris*
32 *Helleborus corsicus*
33 *Fatsia japonica*
34 *Skimmia × foremanii*
35 *Arundinaria nitida*
36 *Geranium endressii*
37 *Parthenocissus henryana*
38 *Festuca glauca*
39 *Mahonia* 'Charity'
40 *Viburnum davidii*
41 *Hosta sieboldiana*

Square Back Gardens

ABOVE *This relatively small garden uses a circular pattern to lead the eye away from rectangular boundaries. The centrepiece is a pool, which has been emphasized by the circular pergola. The latter is constructed from metal which brings with it an inherent lightness. It also acts as a frame to a changing set of views as one moves through the space. The seating arranged around the pool reinforces the circular theme of the whole composition.*

OPPOSITE *Steps drop down to this garden and heighten the feeling of seclusion provided by the surrounding planting. This classic composition has as its focus a central bed within which is set an armillary sphere. Seating is arranged around the edges so that one naturally looks inwards, away from those surrounding boundaries. Gravel has been chosen as a sensible surface – grass is often quite unsuitable in such a small area.*

All design depends on a degree of visual movement. In a garden this is augmented by being able to move through the space, as well as by the vertical height of the walls, the planting and the dimensions of surrounding buildings. The way in which we relate to a garden also depends on its overall dimensions: a long, narrow plot encourages movement from one end to the other, while a dog-leg invites us around a corner. Square gardens, however, are essentially static; no one dimension predominates. In consequence, they are the most difficult to handle. The primary task is to give the composition a feeling of space and movement.

There are two basic ways of handling the problem. The most obvious of these is to employ a circular pattern, turning it upon itself to focus on a specific feature within the garden. This type of design leads the eye away from the rectangular boundaries. The peripheral areas are taken up with planting that softens and surrounds the com-

position. Such planting can be as high as possible along the boundaries, grading gently down, thus reinforcing the visual bias towards the central area. In the centre planting can again be used as a centrepiece. Alternatively a well-chosen piece of statuary or a pool can act as the focal point. There is an obvious circulation pattern around this design.

In a garden of this shape best results can often be achieved by using a pattern that is unashamedly rectangular, reinforcing the basic shape and building upon it. By this I do not mean using a formal pattern. The second approach divides the garden into areas of paving, planting and perhaps water. Think of planning the garden on a grid and then start to rough out what you want to go where. Overlap rectangles, raise areas and emphasize a particular route from door to gate or sitting area. This will produce a totally unique pattern, a pattern that will in all probability be a perfect vehicle for your personal lifestyle.

Of course not all town gardens are small. Many properties have plots of quite reasonable size. This garden measures about 16m (50ft) square and provides considerable scope for a wide range of activities. Because it is difficult to produce a feeling of movement in a square plot, a useful technique is to turn the whole design at an angle to the surrounding boundaries, setting up a diagonal pattern. Such a line

across any rectangle is the longest dimension, so this automatically creates a feeling of greater space. Moving away from the house there is a paved terrace of ample size, constructed from 'brushed' concrete contained within panels of brick. This theme is extended in the brick path that passes underneath the archway, terminating at the second sitting area and conservatory. The path

continues in a curve back to the house. Being set just below the level of the surrounding turf, it also acts as a moving edge, reducing that chore to a minimum. The pool acts as a pivot to the whole design, and this is being reinforced by a bed of pure white floribunda roses. Planting, carefully chosen to provide colour and interest throughout the year, surrounds the garden.

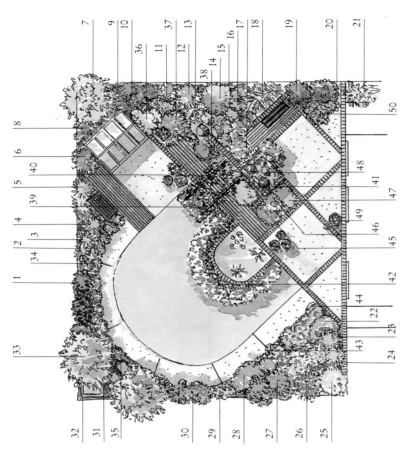

SQUARE GARDEN
PLANT LIST

1 *Berberis thunbergii* 'Atropurpurea'
2 *Clematis tangutica* (ON FENCE)
3 *Cytisus* 'Cornish Cream'
4 *Yucca flaccida*
5 *Miscanthus sinensis* 'Zebrinus'
6 *Syringa microphylla* 'Superba'
7 *Prunus avium*
8 *Arundinaria murieliae*
9 *Clematis montana* var. *wilsonii* (ON WALL)
10 *Elaeagnus × ebbingii* 'Limelight'
11 *Weigela florida* 'Foliis Purpureis'
12 *Hebe* 'Midsummer Beauty'
13 *Salvia officinalis* 'Icterina'
14 *Pyrus salicifolia* 'Pendula'
15 *Vitis vinifera* 'Purpurea' (THROUGH PYRUS)
16 *Rosmarinus* 'Miss Jessop's variety'
17 *Heuchera* 'Palace Purple'
18 *Hemerocallis* 'Dream Waltz'
19 *Choisya ternata*
20 *Hedera colchica* 'Paddy's Pride' (ON FENCE)
21 *Arundinaria viridistriata*
22 *Hebe pinguifolia* 'Pagei'
23 *Hydrangea anomala* subsp. *petiolaris*
24 *Mahonia* 'Charity'
25 *Philadelphus* 'Belle Etoile'
26 *Buddleia davidii* 'Empire Blue'
27 *Cotinus coggygria* 'Royal Purple'
28 *Senecio greyi*
29 *Aristolochia sempervirens*
30 *Ceanothus* 'Burkwoodii'
31 *Potentilla* 'Katherine Dykes'
32 *Lonicera periclymenum* 'Serotina' (ON FENCE & SCREEN)
33 *Betula utilis* subsp. *jaquemontii*
34 *Geranium platypetalum*
35 Drift of *Centaurea dealbata* 'John Coutts'
36 *Euphorbia polychroma*
37 *Cotoneaster microphyllus*
38 *Geranium phaeum*
39 *Avena candida*
40 Climbing roses 'Danse du Feu'
41 *Stachys lanata*
42 Bed of 'Iceberg' floribunda roses
43 *Potentilla* 'Tangerine'
44 *Rosa* 'Nozomi'
45 *Hebe rakaiensis*
46 *Euphorbia wulfenii*
47 Clump of *Origanum vulgare*
48 Raised bed / Collection of Miniature Conifers and Heathers
49 Pot with Clematis 'Nellie Moser'
50 *Bergenia* 'Sunningdale'

RIGHT *Within a garden it is often attractive and desirable to set aside an area with a quite different theme. This sunken terrace has a character of its own, focusing on the central pot.*

Long Narrow Back Gardens

Long, narrow gardens are the most pleasing and rewarding to handle. The problem is that very few people understand the real potential of such gardens; the usual treatment consists of a path down the middle flanked by narrow borders, with further borders echoing the line of the surrounding fences. More often than not the path serves a washing line and ends in a motley collection of garden buildings at the bottom.

Designing such a garden should proceed as with any other — work out what you have got and what you want and then start to rough out just where the different elements should go. The best way to do this is to subdivide the composition into separate areas — the longer the garden, the more 'rooms' you can have. In most cases the main sitting area will adjoin the house and should always be large enough to accommodate a table and chairs. Such areas should be essentially architectural in character. Here is the place for rectangular paving.

In order to avoid the path-straight-down-the-middle syndrome, keep it to one side. It can lead into different rooms, each of which can embrace an individual theme, a particular plant colour scheme or style of garden. One section might be for play, another for salad crops or herbs and yet another for small fruit trees. Each will have a different character and each a different level of maintenance. Surprise is one of the most important elements in garden design and there is ample scope here to divide the rooms with a variety of arches, pergolas, screens, planting or hedges. Try to provide a feeling of continuity between your different 'rooms' by using compatible materials or plants.

If there is a change of level, then so much the better. This can be the perfect vehicle for broad steps which can accommodate the drop. Steps are also perfect punctuation marks in a garden, they are perfect places for a pot or urn or, if there is room, even a seat. If using steps remember the practical problems of moving machinery or wheel barrows. Shallow risers may be satisfactory but more often than not a ramp, which can be set within or to one side of the flight, will be the answer. This too will be of real benefit to the elderly or to children, enabling the latter to make full use of wheeled toys. Ensure there is enough room at the bottom of the ramp to stop or turn and avoid positioning prickly plants here. They could cause a nasty accident if anyone collided with them at speed.

ABOVE *There are two basic ways to handle a long, narrow plot. Either the space can be broken up with different areas of paving and planting or the shape can be emphasized. This garden, designed by Tim Du Val, embraces the latter technique and is formally laid out. Such a pattern is accentuated by the centrally placed table and chairs and is reinforced by the flanking borders, summerhouse and urn.*

OPPOSITE *This classic town garden has been beautifully and confidently handled. The length has been emphasized, but in an asymmetrical fashion rather than a rigidly formal line. Water provides a linking element, reinforced with a long path flanked by planting. Planting also bangs over the water which has been crossed by a simple wooden bridge and the reflections add to the composition.*

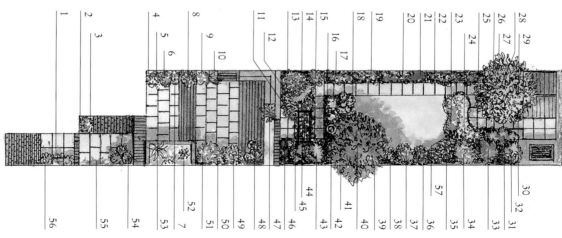

LEFT *A circular movement has been introduced into this long narrow garden by the design of the brick paving. The edges are tempered by overhanging planting and the well-positioned pots.*

1
2
3
4
5
6
8
9
10
11
12
13
14
15
16
17
18
19
20
21
22
23
24
25
26
27
28
29
30
31
32
33
34
35
36
37
38
39
40
41
42
43
44
45
46
47
48
49
50
51
52
53
54
55
56
57

This garden really is the classic long, narrow garden; it is 5m (16ft) wide and just under 33m (100ft) long. A series of sections or rooms has been woven into an interesting interlocking composition. The overall design is essentially architectural, and the two basic paving materials of precast slabs and brick are repeated throughout the garden.

Access is from a back door and french windows that open onto the main terrace area. To make the space feel as wide as possible the paving has been laid in a 'breaking' bond across the garden, the raised pool acting as a delightful focal point that can be seen from all the windows of the house. A built-in seat and barbecue are the practical features while an archway leads into the next room.

LONG NARROW GARDEN PLANT LIST

1 *Bergenia* 'Silberlicht'
2 *Actinidia kolomikta*
3 *Hebe rakaiensis*
4 *Jasminum officinale*
5 Drift of lime green nicotiana
6 *Phlomis fruticosa*
7 *Cytisus* × *kewensis*
8 *Hosta crispula* (IN POT)
9 *Geranium* 'Russell Pritchard'
10 *Rosmarinus* 'Miss Jessop's variety'
11 *Campanula persicifolia*
12 *Senecio greyi*
13 *Hibiscus syriacus* 'Blue Bird'
14 *Lonicera japonica* 'Aureo-Reticulata'
15 *Artemisia absinthium* 'Lambrook Silver'
16 *Genista lydia*
17 *Heuchera* 'Palace Purple'
18 *Santolina chamaecyparissus*
19 *Clematis tangutica*
20 *Lilium regale*
21 *Nepeta* × *faassenii*
22 *Arundinaria viridistriata*
23 *Hebe pinguifolia* 'Pagei'
24 *Alchemilla mollis*
25 × *Fatshedera lizei* 'Variegata'
26 *Anemone* × *hybrida* 'Alba'
27 *Elaeagnus* × *ebbingii* 'Limelight'
28 *Betula utilis* subsp *jaquemontii*
29 *Hydrangea macrophylla* 'Blue Wave'
30 *Geranium endressii*
31 *Skimmia reevesiana*
32 *Fatsia japonica*
33 *Mahonia lomariifolia*
34 *Potentilla* 'Katherine Dykes'
35 *Parthenocissus henryana*
36 *Fuchsia magellanica* 'Versicolor'
37 *Ceanothus* 'Autumnal Blue'
38 *Papaver orientale* 'Mrs Perry'
39 *Spartina pectinata* 'Aureo-Marginata'
40 *Acer griseum*
41 *Acanthus spinosus*
42 Marguerite daisies (IN URN)
43 *Choisya ternata*
44 *Rosa* 'Zéphirine Drouhin' (ARCH)
45 *Caryopteris* × *clandonensis* 'Kew Blue'
46 *Berberis thunbergii* 'Atropurpurea Nana'
47 *Hosta sieboldiana*
48 Californian poppies in pots
49 *Euphorbia wulfenii*
50 *Clematis macropetala*
51 *Cistus* × *cyprius*
52 *Myosotis scorpioides*
53 *Iris pseudacorus* 'Variegata'
54 Herbs in pots
55 *Clematis macropetala*
56 *Hedera helix* 'Gold Heart'
57 *Agapanthus* – Headbourne hybrids

Roof Gardens and Balconies

LIBRARY
GARDEN EDUCATION CENTER
OF GREENWICH

Roof gardens and balconies are in a class of their own. Here special criteria must be considered, especially the load-bearing capacity of the roof. Providing the structure below is up to the strain, and you should always consult an architect or structural engineer if in the slightest doubt, then the possibilities are legion. Remember, too, that the climate will be harsh, with higher than average temperatures and the possibility of strong winds. This will mean that soil will quickly dry out, making irrigation and the selection of plants that can tolerate such conditions important. Don't forget that all materials needed to construct the garden will need to be brought up to the roof, often through an awkward access point. These materials should be as light as possible and one should be thinking of building any raised beds from timber rather than brick or blocks and filling such beds with a lightweight soil mix. The latter can be purchased from any good garden centre and usually incorporates a slow-release fertilizer. Fertility is quickly exhausted in most of such mixes, so regular applications of a liquid feed will be ideal. When using pots ensure that these are sensibly large, again to retain as much moisture as possible. Never place any container on the edge of a roof or balcony where there is the chance of it falling to the street below and injuring somebody.

If shelter is necessary, think of topping walls with trellis or a permeable screen rather than a solid barrier of glass or timber. The latter will create turbulence, whereas the former will tend to filter and reduce the force of a wind.

Conventional slab or stone paving is usually too heavy unless the sub-structure has been designed to bear such loads. Instead, there are a number of lightweight tiles that are particularly suitable. A roof garden is one place where imitation grass, known as Astroturf, can be particularly useful. Think of it as carpet – it looks good and needs no water. It can also be cut to a curve with a pair of scissors – one way to build up a real feeling of movement in a limited space. Chippings are useful to create a subtle contrast to the greenery, and can be thinly spread to minimize weight.

It is a big mistake to use white paint on roof gardens. It is too glaring in the prevailing brighter light conditions – far better to use cream or another muted colour that is easier on the eye and that will complement the colours of your plants.

ABOVE So often we forget the power of the sun on a roof, but these coloured blinds are the perfect answer. This garden's plants are arranged in an interesting collection of containers that appropriately include a chimney pot. In this garden and the one on the opposite page, small scale paving increases the intimacy of the space. Small tiles are also usually light in weight and reduce the load that has to be carried by the roof below.

OPPOSITE In this garden designed by Tim Du Val we see the best elements of roof gardening brought together in a single composition. There is screening that both filters the wind and acts as a host to climbing plants, there are ample pots that allow a generous root run for largely evergreen species and there is room enough for sitting and dining. Above all, the view is what it should be – superb.

Roof Gardens

This is a purpose-built roof garden of quite generous proportions. In its original state it was entirely floored with small grey lightweight tiles and the brief was to produce something far more interesting which would emphasize the dramatic city views. A pattern of overhead beams that cast shade and deflected the glare of the sun was introduced. Decking overlays the tiles and echoes the beams above. A built-in seat acts as a pivot to the garden as a whole. Automatic irrigation was also fitted to ease maintenance.

Stepping stones cross an area of cream gravel chippings, giving access to the existing tiles and the sweeping 'lawn' or Astroturf. This shape is reflected in the raised bed, which is planted with drought-tolerant species and built from wooden slats bolted to curved metal formers.

One important consideration on any roof garden is to maintain any drainage outlets or gullies. In this garden the drain lies beneath the timber deck, which provides the perfect disguise.

ABOVE LEFT *You can see the difference between a roof left bare and one planted with a collection of shrubs. The rose is particularly spectacular but would need regular feeding to maintain such healthy growth. The selection of a chestnut can only be a temporary measure, as this will quickly outstrip any container.*

LEFT *This charming little roof garden cleverly belies its size with a collection of well-planted pots. The adjoining roof is disguised by a neat trellis and a raised bed.*

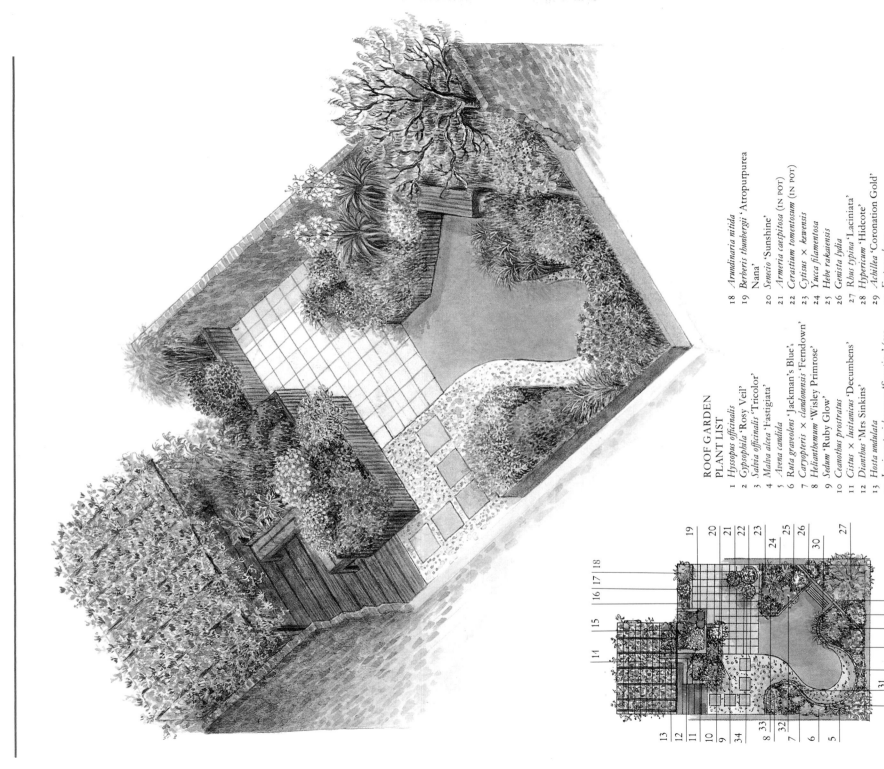

ROOF GARDEN
PLANT LIST

1 *Hyssopus officinalis*
2 *Gypsophila* 'Rosy Veil'
3 *Salvia officinalis* 'Tricolor'
4 *Malva alcea* 'Fastigiata'
5 *Avena candida*
6 *Ruta graveolens* 'Jackman's Blue',
7 *Caryopteris × clandonensis* 'Ferndown',
8 *Helianthemum* 'Wisley Primrose'
9 *Sedum* 'Ruby Glow'
10 *Ceanothus prostratus*
11 *Cistus × lusitanicus* 'Decumbens'
12 *Dianthus* 'Mrs Sinkins'
13 *Hosta undulata*
14 *Lonicera periclymenum* 'Serotina' (ON BEAMS)
15 *Lavandula vera*
16 *Clematis montana* 'Tetrarose'
17 *Potentilla* 'Tangerine'
18 *Arundinaria nitida*
19 *Berberis thunbergii* 'Atropurpurea Nana'
20 *Senecio* 'Sunshine'
21 *Armeria caespitosa* (IN POT)
22 *Cerastium tomentosum* (IN POT)
23 *Cytisus × kewensis*
24 *Yucca filamentosa*
25 *Hebe rakaiensis*
26 *Genista lydia*
27 *Rhus typina* 'Laciniata'
28 *Hypericum* 'Hidcote'
29 *Achillea* 'Coronation Gold'
30 *Festuca glauca*
31 *Thymus serpyllum* 'Albus'
32 *Nepeta mussini*
33 *Helianthemum* 'Wisley Pink'
34 Night-scented stocks (IN POT)

Balconies

Balconies are in many ways like tiny courtyards. Space is always at a premium and this usually means that there is little or no room to build complicated structures or raised beds. As with roof gardens there are problems of heat, drought and an often fierce wind, and the lack of space means that pots may have to be small. More often than not the sides of a balcony are partitioned off with a blank

wall or screen to provide privacy. This may provide support for a well-worked trellis or wires that can be used to support a variety of tough climbing plants. The front of the balcony will probably form a retaining wall and it is often possible to top this with a series of troughs or window boxes. Always make sure that these are securely fixed and fill them with a lightweight compost mix.

Free-standing pots will also be useful and in this garden they have been planted with a selection of mixed shrubs and climbers, including a fine tree and a number of herbs.

Plants in the troughs have been selected for their ability to flop over the edges and soften the parapet wall. They are also virtually maintenance-free, forming a dense carpet once established.

ABOVE A tiny balcony uses a series of well-anchored window boxes to act as host to roses and pretty white daisies. Such treatment softens an otherwise austere scene, bringing colour and a breath of country air to an urban street.

RIGHT This balcony has a partition wall dividing it from the adjoining building, providing an ideal host for a purpose-built trellis which has been echoed on the main wall of the house. Tim Du V al, the designer, has cleverly disguised the boundaries to create a feeling of greater space.

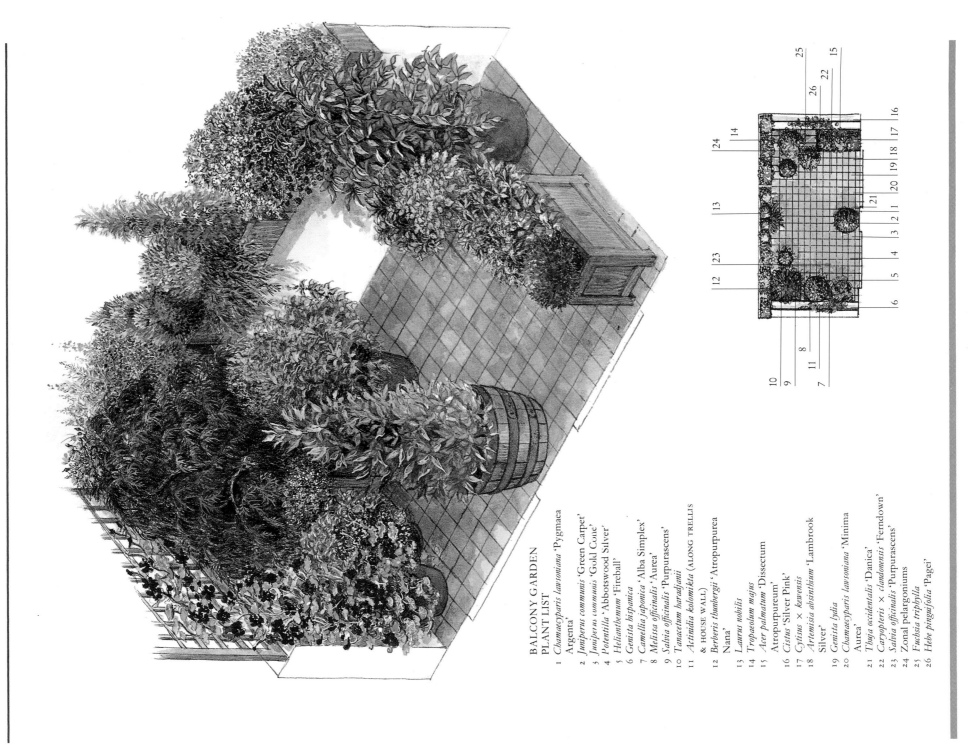

BALCONY GARDEN
PLANT LIST

1 Chamaecyparis lawsoniana 'Pygmaea
   Argenta'
2 Juniperus communis 'Green Carpet'
3 Juniperus communis 'Gold Cone'
4 Potentilla 'Abbotswood Silver'
5 Helianthemum 'Fireball'
6 Genista hispanica
7 Camellia japonica 'Alba Simplex'
8 Melissa officinalis 'Aurea'
9 Salvia officinalis 'Purpurascens'
10 Tanacetum haradjanii
11 Actinidia kolomikta (ALONG TRELLIS
   & HOUSE WALL)
12 Berberis thunbergii 'Atropurpurea
   Nana'
13 Laurus nobilis
14 Tropaeolum majus
15 Acer palmatum 'Dissectum
   Atropurpureum'
16 Cistus 'Silver Pink'
17 Cytisus × kewensis
18 Artemisia absinthium 'Lambrook
   Silver'
19 Genista lydia
20 Chamaecyparis lawsoniana 'Minima
   Aurea'
21 Thuja occidentalis 'Danica'
22 Caryopteris × clandonensis 'Ferndown'
23 Salvia officinalis 'Purpurascens'
24 Zonal pelargoniums
25 Fuchsia triphylla
26 Hebe pinguifolia 'Pagei'

FURNISHINGS AND ORNAMENTS

The conception, design and construction of a garden is a rewarding and worthwhile undertaking, bringing together all those essential aspects of hard and soft landscape. The final choice of ornamentation, however, is rather different, allowing one to inject considerable personality into the overall composition. By this time you should have a real understanding of your outside room — you will know its good and awkward points, you will know just where the sun rises and sets, the direction of a prevailing wind and the line of a neighbour's window. As with all the other aspects of garden design, ornamentation should be chosen with your goal of minimal maintenance firmly in mind. You should not, for example, choose furniture which needs frequent treatment to withstand extremes of temperature. The ideas here should ensure your work level will be reduced.

Like any room inside the house, much of the hard work of preparation is concealed beneath well-built structures and surfaces. Outside, of course, the wall coverings are more often than not of living matter, with the texture and colour of foliage blending with flower and stem to provide interest throughout the year. But a garden has to be more than the paving, planting and walling that forms the basic framework. All of this may look fine, but when it comes down to it, your room outside needs to 'work' and not simply form a pretty backdrop.

Furnishings are therefore vital, to bring the space alive in terms of intimacy and to act as

ABOVE *Ornaments are often the very essence of town gardens and here planting and pot complement each other beautifully.*

OPPOSITE *This is the ultimate town garden, a real outside room. The floor is a combination of brick paving and fine old stone, pots and paving tempering the outline. Trellis divides the space, the statue drawing the eye and forming a focal point.*

movable components, in opposition to the static ones that form the remainder of the underlying pattern in your garden.

There are extremes in garden ornamentation — such as when the whole garden becomes an ornament in its own right. This sort of approach is not easy to handle and should only be contemplated if you are prepared to live with something that is both stylized and difficult to change. The ultimate example, which can just work in a small urban garden, is the creation of a chessboard. This can be achieved with contrasting paving or decking and, if done properly, on a large enough scale, the end result can be spectacular. The secret is strength of purpose; there can be no compromise. To try and fit such a design into half a garden spells visual disaster.

A second drastic idea, and one that I worked on in a quite tiny New York garden, was an inside-to-out swimming pool. This took up over half the ground floor and could be separated from the garden by a combination of a motorized glass panel and, when open, an air curtain. The engineering problems were expensive, but were solved with a large amount of structural underpinning and dehumidification. The end result was quite stunning when people and moving water brought the composition alive. The garden walls were formed of mirrors, the planting kept to large-leaved climbers that engendered a subtropical feel. At night, with underwater lighting, the result was nothing short of magical.

Outdoor living

A good building, whether it be a conservatory, shed or greenhouse, should be both practical and good-looking. We looked at the basic merits of various buildings earlier in the book but it is worth underlining the essential fact that any structure should reflect the style of architecture it adjoins. If there is nothing suitable that can be purchased 'off the peg', then it may be worth having something purpose-built for you. This applies particularly to conservatories because the trend towards 'period' buildings has produced an uncomfortable rash of structures that are far from visually compatible with their surroundings. Planting will do much to integrate any building into the fabric of the garden both at ground level or grown onto wires attached to the building itself. The addition of any structure to a garden will also change the circulation pattern, so allow ample paved areas for sitting and construct sensible paths for access.

Eating outside, provided the weather is kind, is one of life's greatest culinary experiences. The smell of barbecued food does much to rouse even the most timid appetite.

Barbecues are big business these days and the range is enormous. In basic terms, there are two alternatives: a built-in model that can become part of the garden framework, or a free-standing type. The former will obviously need to be thought about early on in the design stage. The position of the allocated area is important: you may want to catch the last rays of the sun in the evening and probably don't want to be too far from the kitchen. The direction of a prevailing wind may also be important: food may smell good but smoke being blown over can be a problem.

Portable barbecues come in all shapes and sizes and you have the ability to move them around. Once again, technology has made cooking outside a lot simpler and many portables accommodate a gas bottle beneath the burners.

OPPOSITE *Garden buildings should blend into a design and in town, where space is limited, this is particularly important. Try and make sure materials used for any structure link with those of the adjoining house and where possible use planting boldly to disguise the inevitably architectural outline. Leave room around the sides to allow for maintenance or repair.*

LEFT *This little cat house is a visual joke in the best possible taste. The thatch is traditional and watertight while the two topiary tails emphasize the point of the whole composition.*

BELOW *You either love or hate barbecuing and if you fall into the former category then it can be well worth building the real thing. It should be sensibly sited to catch the late afternoon sun and preferably close to the kitchen.*

Any activity outside is dependent on the weather, both good and bad. In the case of a barbecue a simple overhead structure of beams, clothed with climbers, can cast a degree of welcome shade on a hot day. Alternatively, if the beams are left clear of foliage, and built to a well-detailed architectural pattern that perhaps picks up the line of decking or fencing below, then a simple tarpaulin can be thrown over the top to prevent both glare and the occasional shower. There is obviously scope here to create a colourway of exterior fabrics, the overhead sheeting echoing the pattern of cushions and the fabric of gaily patterned canvas chairs. Take this a stage further and you can link the colour scheme back indoors, to a playroom, kitchen or lounge.

Sun, even in a temperate climate, can be a real problem, because of its bleaching action on materials indoors. With the advent of large glassed-in areas, this has been accentuated and some method of shading should be incorporated. There are a number of filter blinds that you can drop down behind the window but more often than not these look less than perfect. I would rather see a well-designed fabric blind, or if well constructed, an outside awning that can be lowered to cut out the worst of the sun's rays. Styles with flounced edges and floral patterns are popular with many garden centres and catalogues but these could be overpowering in many urban gardens. Some awnings are motorized, which is terrific when they work. A simple pulley

FAR LEFT *Overhead beams help to define a sitting area, casting light shade and providing the ideal host for climbing plants. A dining table can be left outside permanently if given adequate protection.*

LEFT *Umbrellas are essential to reduce glare when eating outside, particularly if tables and chairs are white. Make sure they are well anchored against wind.*

BELOW *Hammocks are the perfect way to spend a lazy summer's afternoon. Remember the prime rule that you should never be a slave to a garden. Do make sure the fixings are adequate and check the ropes for rot at regular intervals.*

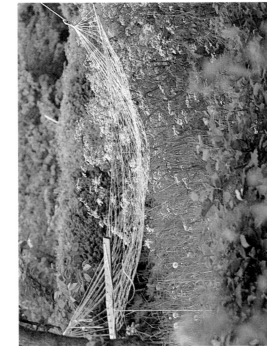

secure points. They take a little getting used to, particularly getting in and out, but there is nothing more relaxing on a summer's day than a hammock-bound snooze with the sound of water playing in the background and the rustle of a breeze through your well-planned foliage. This is what gardening is all about – remember the golden rule that you should never be a slave to your room outside.

Hammocks can easily be moved from place to place, chasing sun or shade, and have the great advantage of taking up virtually no space when taken down and stowed away. For safety's sake, always check the condition of fabric and, more importantly, the securing ropes. Rot-proof nylon provides the safest material.

system that can be roped to a cleat is workmanlike and sensible – and cheaper.

Any fabric in the garden will be vulnerable to the weather and, although awnings and tarpaulins will almost certainly be made from water-repellent material or a plasticized weave, check that canvas chairs are also proofed. Cushions can be quickly scooped up in the case of a shower but chairs and loungers will more often than not have to stand outside until the rain is over. Most manufacturers ensure waterproof fabrics for cushions too, but if you make them up yourself, be sure to select an appropriate material.

Hammocks can become quite indispensable in a tiny town garden, and can be slung from any two

Furniture

I have mentioned the possibility of built-in seating adjoining a barbecue – a cost-effective and practical idea. This same theme can be used elsewhere and a raised bed or pool can be constructed with a wide coping that will double as an occasional seat. Right angles formed by the junction of two walls can often form an awkward corner, but again, with a combination of a built-in timber seat and either raised or ground-level planting, one can create a delightful composition. Timber is the most sensible material for the top and, if this is fitted or hinged from a sturdy brick base, then the unit doubles as invaluable storage space, always more than welcome in a small garden.

Trees can be a mixed blessing in an urban scene, on the one hand dropping vast quantities of leaves, on the other providing an excellent screen from adjoining buildings. A mature tree can also act as the perfect host to a built-in seat and there is a

chance here to reinforce the basic ground plan with either a rectangular or circular pattern. Such a seat can do a number of things: it can cover up that awkward run of roots that radiates out from the trunk and, if built large enough, double as both table and seating area. Build it with a timber rather than a brick base, as the bricks are more subject to soil heave from the roots and will quickly crack. Paint it to pick up a colour scheme on the house or stain it with a preservative. The latter will involve rather less annual maintenance. Think in terms of something at least 1.8m (6ft) square and have plenty of scatter cushions handy.

Remember too that trees are very much a haven for wildlife in the city and a well-placed nesting-box in addition to the thoughtful provision of food and water will give you many hours of pleasure. Bird-tables and baths come in as many types as their users; well sited, they can become an excellent focal point, but don't forget that cats can be a serious problem in towns. The cost and maintenance of such a feature are minimal, but the returns in visual and ecological terms are considerable.

The range of furniture on the market is both enormous and appalling. While cost is, of course, a factor, it is no excuse to manufacture low-priced, poorly built rubbish when a little thought would have produced a well-designed article at approximately the same price. Economy furniture inside the home has undergone a revolution over the past few years and one can choose from a vast range. It is a great pity that this same trend has as yet made very little headway in the room outside.

With all good design you need to respect the underlying theme and pattern of your garden. The incongruity of a flimsy bent-wire table and chairs against a backdrop of solid wrought-iron railings should be self-evident, but it is common enough. What could be more natural here than a similar set of wrought-iron (or good alloy imitation) furniture that reflects the underlying mood of the composition. A similar approach would be to use well-designed timber furniture on a deck or in a situation that used timber overheads or screening.

In town gardens there is often a limitation on space and storage, and maintenance of any object needs to be kept to a sensible minimum. Most furniture may have to be left out throughout the year, calling for sound construction and rot-proof materials. Most timber garden furniture is relatively

ABOVE *As with rooms inside the house try and work to a particular theme. Here timber decking is also used for seating at a higher level. The deck chair has the added benefit of easy storage during the winter.*

OPPOSITE *Stone furniture is often stronger on visual appeal than practicality. I find lions ostentatious but the planting saves the day, softening the lines.*

OPPOSITE There is something about this composition of alternately positioned seating that has great charm. It defines the two separate garden rooms, planting reinforcing the division. Such planting has been carefully chosen so that when sitting the sight-line is broken, enhancing a feeling of greater space. Fragrance and the choice of plants that whisper in the breeze are ideal in this situation.

BELOW In any garden the transition between inside and out should be as inconspicuous as possible. These sliding glass doors are perfect, while the furniture is simple and well chosen and don't forget that a pot adds interest when the surface is not in use. If table and chairs are positioned to match the lines of paving or the house they inevitably look more comfortable.

heavy and bulky. If constructed from hardwood such as teak or iroko and treated once a year with a preservative oil, it will have a long and useful life. Collapsible tables and chairs, constructed entirely in wood or in part timber and part canvas, can be much cheaper although, due to their lighter construction, they would have to be stowed away during cold or wet weather.

The fashion of combined 'campsite' tables with built-in seating seems to have lost favour recently. It is true that this type of furniture is hardly elegant, but it is tough and can take up a relatively small space. If you are designing your garden from scratch, then it may be worth thinking about a permanent site for such furniture. Such a style goes well with decking and an adjoining timber house.

Plastic furniture has improved in recent years and, although there is still plenty of sub-standard material around, some designs are quite superb. With a little care in shopping around you can find reasonable furniture at a reasonable price. Several manufacturers sell fully co-ordinated sets that have removable cushions and parasols, while the furniture itself is designed to be left outside throughout the winter. Such furniture is virtually maintenance-free and, while it does not automatically look good in every garden, it can be successfully used in most, particularly when you have a wide range of fabrics to choose from to blend it into a backdrop of planting and interior colour scheme.

When making a choice remember to get a table of ample size. Meals on the patio tend to be more relaxed and take up more space than dining inside the house. It is also worth bearing in mind that a patio or paved area needs to be at least 3.6m (12ft) square if it is to accommodate an adequately-sized table and chairs comfortably.

Finally, don't forget the value of using a single well-positioned bench or seat as a focal point. This can be particularly effective to draw the eye in a certain direction and allows the opportunity to provide an alternative sitting area, perhaps sited in a shady corner rather than the full sun of the main patio. A white seat is particularly striking in a shady courtyard surrounded by lush, largely evergreen planting, providing a real punctuation mark within the overall setting. Remember though that a focal point is just that, so choose that seat carefully. This is one place where you will very obviously get what you pay for and be aware of your choice constantly.

Pots and containers

The value of pots and containers in a city garden is enormous, not only in providing a growing medium in sometimes almost impossible situations but also in their capacity of enabling instant colour to be injected. The range of containers is vast. As in the other elements of garden design, try to remain constant to a theme. In other words, don't mix plastic pots with terracotta or stone, however attractive these are in their own right. A garden that uses mainly natural materials in its construction should echo these in its furnishings. Likewise, a contemporary, crisp design using synthetics will readily accept plastic, metal or fibreglass. Remember, too, that in many instances the container

becomes almost incidental, with foliage spilling out over the sides to completely disguise the pot below.

The way in which pots are grouped also affects the overall garden design. A single pot placed with care can form an attractive focal point. When using more than one container stick to odd numbers: two and four look awkward but three and five comfortable. Vary the heights and sizes of pots in a setting to build up an interesting composition.

Certain materials can also be damaged by frost, in particular terracotta and reconstituted stone pots. More often than not these have been imported from a frost-free country where this problem does not occur. Check their durability before purchase or you may be in for an expensive shock.

As a general rule the larger and deeper a container the happier the plants will be as they will have a more generous root run and stand longer intervals between irrigation. This latter point is particularly pertinent if you plan to go away on holiday. Neighbours are not always forthcoming for watering duty and it can be a tragedy to return to bone-dry pots and dead plants. This is one instance where automatic irrigation can be of real value.

Many unlikely containers, including old washhouse tubs, coal scuttles, porcelain or stone sinks and even buckets, make excellent homes for plants. Half-barrels are another low-cost, sensible choice. They are extremely durable and eminently suitable for shrubs of considerable size, including fruit trees

BELOW LEFT Hanging baskets can provide instant colour in a variety of situations. Remember they need regular watering and feeding.

BELOW Pots can be used very successfully as focal points – here the simply textured pot stands out against sculptured foliage.

OPPOSITE The bigger the pot the better it will be for a plant, allowing ample root room. Larger pots also have the added advantage of less frequent watering for the plant – thus saving on maintenance time for you. When choosing pots it can be useful to keep to a single material of, say, terracotta to provide continuity.

grown on a 'dwarfing' root-stock. If using any of these, be sure to incorporate drainage holes or the soil will become waterlogged and eventually sour.

Another advantage of containers, as with raised beds, is the ability to vary the acidity of the soil so that one can grow those cherished camellias or azaleas in a garden which is otherwise solid chalk. You could also enjoy the pleasures of both blue and pink hydrangeas, blue enjoying an acid environment, pink preferring alkaline.

Although you can use ordinary garden soil in a pot, it is worth bearing in mind that this may be full of pests and diseases and be very heavy – a problem if you have to move containers around or if they are standing on a roof or balcony. If you use a potting compost this will contain sterile loam and a balanced fertilizer. Very lightweight composts can be obtained for hanging baskets and window boxes. These often contain a water-retentive gel but such a mixture will be quickly exhausted by plants and will need regular watering as well as liquid feeding.

Because of the size of pots and the subsequent loss of nutrition, it is best to maintain big containers annually by removing approximately 15cm (6in) of compost and replacing this with fresh, incorporating a general fertilizer at the same time. It does not take long and the result is renewed vigour.

Just what you grow in containers is very much up to you, but with regular feeding and watering the range is virtually limitless.

Statues and ornaments

Just what makes a statue or ornament acceptable really depends on individual taste. Brightly coloured gnomes are considered so appalling by some as to bring on an instant headache. But don't become a gardening snob – if you want a gnome – and they come in all shapes, sizes and degrees of garishness – then by all means have one, or a family of them. Gardening is after all fun, and as soon as you remove that essential sense of humour the whole exercise becomes dull.

A trip round any garden centre will offer figures of every size and description from incontinent cherubs to stalking cats. In broad terms you get what you pay for and, while galleries and up-market art dealers offer items at horrendous prices, there are many well-made reproduction items at a fair price. Many of these are offered through catalogues and, because of the size and weight of the larger pieces, they are not often available through the average retail outlet. So it is worth shopping around. As a designer I try to discourage my clients asking me to choose ornaments for them. This is, after all, a very personal business and can change the whole emphasis and style of a composition. As a general rule, you do not find a good piece by going out and

looking for it – it will find you, tucked away in some shop or perhaps even in an auction. When you see it, you will know it is for you and also the exact place where it should be sited.

Do not automatically think ornaments have to be a figure of some kind. A large, empty, glazed pot, an old broken column or even a large, smooth boulder are all ornaments in their own right. What is important is their relationship to the overall garden plan and their rightness for you.

OPPOSITE *The choice of a statue is highly personal and can say much about the owner of a garden. Styles range from classical to contemporary while the materials in which pieces are made are equally diverse.*

BELOW *Pots need not contain plants and if of a sufficiently sculptural size and shape can stand alone in splendid isolation.*

BELOW LEFT *Few people would recognize this as an 'armillary sphere' which was an early representation of a celestial globe.*

Lighting

It is a great pity that gardens are so little used during the hours of darkness. We have already seen that a city garden has great advantages in terms of shelter and higher average night-time temperatures. The key to all this is sensitive garden lighting. The prime rule of illumination outdoors is the provision of adequate but simple light.

Garden lighting is split into two broad areas: utilitarian and decorative. The first of these is concerned with the simple matter of clearly lighting points of access from the house, including drives, paths, steps and sitting areas. This category also includes security lighting, always an important factor in an urban environment. Such lighting is always something of a problem as by its very nature it needs to illuminate clearly as large an area as possible. This obviously tends to kill a more subtle scheme and so the best approach is to have such lighting on a separate circuit that can be switched on independently when you are out or away from the property and want it to look as if you're in.

Light fittings need to blend into a setting rather than become focal points in their own right. The pseudo coach lamps which are currently fashionable rarely look successful. Imitation standard gas lamps also fall into this category. They were intended for streets and while real ones are just about all right in a large expanse of drive, in a small urban garden imitation ones almost inevitably look pretentious. There are enough good modern fittings to allow a sensible choice.

The positioning of lamps should be reasonably obvious and, as a general rule, a number of low-wattage bulbs do a better and less spectacular job than a single whopper. Lighting for steps is particularly important and it can be worthwhile building lights into the sides of the flight or even recessed into the risers. Light will therefore be cast where it is needed and not, as is so often the case, on the top of one's head.

Decorative lighting demands a completely different technique. The appeal of a good scheme is a combination of simplicity and subtlety. It is also worth remembering that daylight produces illumination from above, meaning that we rarely get a chance to see plant material or other constituent parts of the garden lit from below. Foliage in particular is quite stunning back- or bottom-lit, and by creating pools of illumination in various well-chosen parts of the garden we create a new

dimension and a longer period in which to enjoy the garden as a whole. Don't forget that lights can be concealed in trees or within garden buildings, shining down onto a statue or other focal point.

Most lighting systems are completely safe to use and many operate off low voltage from a transformer in the house. Fully waterproofed bulbs are fitted onto ground spikes that can be positioned at will and there are also fittings that can be neatly clipped onto the branch of a tree. Such systems need little or no maintenance, but be sure you know where the cables run so as not to chop them in half

with a spade. If you are in any doubt about where the cables in your garden are consult a professional electrician; his fee may well be worth it.

The colour of bulbs is another bone of contention and once again they come in all hues. As a rule keep clear of red, orange and green – these simply turn foliage a revolting colour. Blue and white are by far the best, making a positive contribution to the overall garden. Lights in pools are particularly important. It is desperately important to keep these simple. The rotating kind with different colours are to be avoided at all costs.

ABOVE LEFT *Lighting in a garden not only extends the time you can enjoy living outside but can give plants and foliage a whole new dimension. The golden rule is simplicity: remember it is the actual light rather than the fitting that is important.*

ABOVE *Lighting around a house serves two main functions, one to make access easier by highlighting doors, parking areas, paths and any changes of level and the second as a deterrent to burglars. In visual terms a number of well-positioned fittings look better than a single glaring bulb.*

LABOUR-SAVING GARDENING

Perhaps the most important criterion for any garden is that it should offer no more work than you can reasonably undertake. Busy people have little time to spare, and being a slave to that room outside, however attractive it may look, is guaranteed quickly to dampen any initial enthusiasm. If this happens, things go downhill fast and, once past the point of no return, both the will and the available time to rectify matters have gone for ever. Of course, if you happen to be a keen gardener then you can gear your workload accordingly, but if you are not then it is essential to plan things to offer the minimum maintenance from the very start.

It is perhaps this element of forward planning that is the key to the whole matter. We saw at the beginning of the design process that, by analyzing what was in the garden and preparing lists of what was wanted, it would be possible to ensure the final composition suited the whole family in the most practical way.

In broad terms, a simple design not only looks the best, but is also far easier to look after. A convoluted pattern, prepared with little thought to the final outcome, will be visually disruptive, continually hard on the pocket and in all probability a drawback if you wish to sell your house. As with the rooms inside the house, there is

ABOVE *Containers are ideal in paved areas and if well planted can provide interest throughout the year.*

OPPOSITE *Any garden is a combination of hard and soft landscape features. If these are well planned then maintenance can be kept to a very sensible minimum. Where relatively large areas of paving are used, plants will be doubly important to soften the outline.*

always a degree of ongoing maintenance. Most of these jobs will need carrying out on a regular basis – some, such as mowing the lawn in summer, every week, others, which might include pruning certain shrubs, once a year.

To make your life much easier, it is worth drawing up a maintenance guide, broken down into the basic areas of hard and soft landscape. This could list everything within and including the boundaries and indicate what to do when. A number of companies now offer computerized garden planning services that detail every plant in the garden, including eventual size, time of flowering, what attention will be needed and when. They also cover lawn care and constructional guidelines. This sort of enlightened garden planning is doing much to revolutionize the way we think about the outside room. Perhaps most importantly, it takes the mystery out of what has been described quite wrongly by many professionals as a difficult subject.

It will be sensible when looking at maintenance to take the subjects in the order they have appeared in this book. This means starting with the hard landscape elements of the garden that include walling, fencing, paving and other structures and then moving onto the soft landscape elements that are concerned with planting.

Hard Landscape

The key to keeping maintenance of all hard landscape features to a minimum is sound construction in the first place. Walls, fences and paving that are built and laid properly may account for much of the initial budget, but it will be well worth it in time saved during later years.

WALLS

Of course you may not have built all the features from scratch and there may well be a time when you need to replace certain items because of ageing and wear and tear. With walls, the most important item is the provision of sound coping that will protect the brick or stone below from the worst of water and frost. Sometimes this coping can be made from a different material than the wall – an engineering brick topping a softer brick below or perhaps a precast concrete or tile coping for a stone wall. Each of these will give the design a slightly different feel, but it should be remembered that one always needs to respect the underlying character of the garden and the surrounding locality.

The joints of brick and most stone walls will be pointed. On older walls pointing was often made up with a lime mortar which deteriorates over the years and eventually crumbles away altogether. Before the wall reaches this unsafe stage it is wise to rake the joints out to a depth of 15mm ($\frac{5}{8}$in) and repoint with a new mortar mix of six parts soft sand, one part cement and one part plasticizer. Dampen the wall in sections about 1m (3ft) square and put in the vertical joints first. Pointing can

be flush, weathered at an angle or keyed. The latter often looks best and is achieved by rubbing each joint back with a short piece of plastic hose pipe or an old bucket handle. Always work neatly and avoid smearing mortar on the face of the wall.

If a wall has already become unsafe, it may also be necessary to build buttresses at regular intervals to provide added strength. If materials are carefully matched, these can become a feature in their own right, the line being extended out into an adjoining border with a wing of hedging or perhaps acting as a point of emphasis for a series of well-chosen ornaments.

Retaining walls need checking from time to time and should always be constructed with a vertical layer of hardcore behind them. Weep holes should also be

Walls are the finest boundaries a garden can have. As a backdrop they are superb and this seat forms an ideal focal point, fitting comfortably between the wings of planting to either side.

incorporated at the bottom to remove excess water. If a wall is not built in this way then the pressure behind it in wet weather can be enormous, quite enough in many instances to cause structural problems. If there is any sign of this, the remedial work just described should be carried out as soon as possible. Raised beds should be treated in much the same way. Remember that raised beds built against a house wall will almost certainly cause problems with rising damp should the damp-proof course be bridged. Always leave a gap between such beds and an adjoining wall.

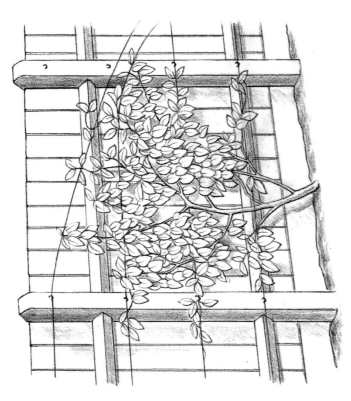

Wire is an ideal, easy support for climbers. Make sure that the branches are securely tied.

Raised beds are often used on roof gardens. Here the degree of work to get plants, materials and soil up several flights of stairs is considerable. To reduce effort and minimize the load on the structure below, use a lightweight compost mixture that contains a percentage of vermiculite. Such composts are usually readily available in pre-packed form.

FENCES

Fences have a shorter life than walls but can nevertheless last a long time if cared for correctly. Any timber in the garden, unless pre-preserved, needs regular treatment with a non-toxic preservative. This will involve carefully taking down any climbers that have helped to soften the outline – which can be a tedious job. To make matters much easier it is a good idea to train plants onto horizontal wires that are stretched between each fence post. If the wire is threaded through galvanized hooks, it can be released easily and the whole plant, on its wire supports, laid flat on the ground. This same technique of wiring can be used on a boundary wall or on the house. It not only looks a good deal neater than trellis, but dispenses with the time-consuming chore of maintaining the latter. Wire is also far more cost-effective and, since it is virtually invisible, the plant, rather than a clutter of woodwork behind, can be more easily admired.

The most vulnerable points of a fence are the top and the bottom, so always fit capping to both the bottom of the posts and the top of the panels themselves.

There should always be a gravel board at the bottom which can be easily renewed in the event of any rot setting in. Concrete posts will not rot, but they do look unsightly. Instead, it can be a good idea to fit concrete spurs that project some 45cm (18in) above the ground, onto which the posts can be bolted. Alternatively, old timber posts can be sawn off near ground level and the sound upper sections bolted to the concrete spurs.

Vertically boarded fences use arris rails between the posts into which the slats are nailed. A vulnerable point is the joint between rail and post. This can be repaired by sawing off the rail flush with the post and fitting a special galvanized steel bracket. A similar fitting can be used to splice two halves of a broken rail together. As a general rule, hardwoods, (oak, elm, cedar, etc.) have a longer life expectancy than softwoods

(pine), although they are correspondingly more expensive. All timber should have been pressure-treated with preservative before purchase.

Trellis uses a combination of heavier supporting timbers and an infill of lighter, more delicate slats. Although it may look pretty, coming in many guises from arbours to garden screens, trellis can be particularly vulnerable. It is also difficult to undo climbers that have woven a tracery through the feature, meaning that, more often than not, large areas do not receive ongoing maintenance at all. This being the case, pre-treated timber is essential. It is worth bearing in mind that such structures need maintenance and have a relatively short life.

This drive has sunk under the weight of passing wheels. The undulating pattern sets up a gentle rhythm that is still smooth enough to be perfectly safe — so no repair is necessary!

within the paving or into adjoining planted areas. Regularly check to see that gullies are kept clear of leaves and other debris. Always look at the position of manholes and drains in relation to any paved area in case access is needed at any time.

Apart from seeing that a paved area is sound, also ensure that slabs, bricks and any other modules employed are neatly pointed. This will not only help to set off the overall pattern but will also mean that it will be virtually impossible for weeds to colonize the joints. In some instances joints between slabs are left open on purpose for the introduction of sprawling plants such as thyme or alchemilla. Remember, however, that grass and other weeds colonize just as quickly as the desired plants and you may have the tedious chore

PAVING

A terrace or patio of ample size will be worth its weight in gold, but it will probably receive more wear and tear than any other single element in the garden. Sound construction is therefore essential to ensure a long life. Many books simply suggest laying paving, of whatever kind, on sand, but although this is a cheap and easy method, the slabs quickly become undermined,

leading to dangerous and uneven surfaces. Paving should be laid over a sound base of well-compacted hardcore and bedded either on a continuous bed or at least spots of mortar. Always ensure that the finished surface is kept 15cm (6in) below the house damp-proof course and also make sure that the area is run to a slight fall to allow water to drain away quickly. This can either be directed into gullies set

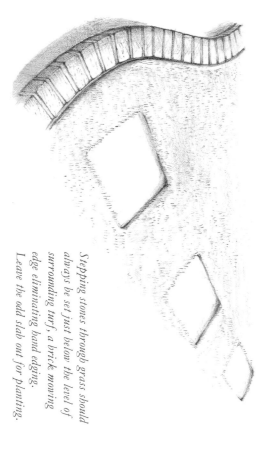

Stepping stones through grass should always be set just below the level of surrounding turf, a brick mowing edge eliminating hand edging. Leave the odd slab out for planting.

of removing them. Open joints also allow the penetration of water and, if it freezes, considerable damage due to frost heave may be caused. If you do have a weed problem, then an application of weedkiller may be necessary. Never keep this in any bottle or container that may look as if it might be used for food or drink. All chemicals should be kept under lock and key in a place well out of the reach of children. Chemicals such as aminotriazole and sodium chlorate are suitable for paths and paving, including gravel, but remember that they are death to plants and should be kept well away from them. Always keep a separate watering can for their application.

It is also worth washing a paved area down in spring and autumn. Use either salt or a suitable cleaner purchased from a garden centre. This will prevent the surface becoming slippery, particularly if it is in shade for much of the day.

PATHS

Paths will need the same attention as paving. Remember to keep stepping stones through grass lower than the turf for easy mowing. A path around a lawn also acts as a mowing edge, preventing damage to overhanging plants and eliminating hand edging, a real maintenance-saver. Simply neaten the grass margin up once a year with a sharp spade or half-moon iron.

STEPS

All steps should be built so that water drains off them quickly, preventing a potential death trap

in winter. If using railway sleepers or other solid baulks of timber, it may be neccessary, particularly in a shady place, to cover the surface with a fine wire mesh. This will be virtually invisible but will provide a non-slip surface at all times.

DECKING

Ventilation below the surface is essential, and all timber should be treated with a preservative regularly. In a damp climate surfaces do not always dry out fully and consequently become

Steps form fascinating patterns, particularly with light and shade but timber can quickly become slippery if they are not scrubbed when algae begins to form.

slippery. Salt can again be used to eliminate this. Boards can also twist and split so always over-order when building the feature, allowing a few lengths to be stored outside to weather down at a similar rate. This will mean a close match can be made if repairs are necessary.

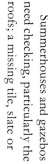

BUILDINGS

Conservatories, sheds and even small greenhouses are useful in an urban garden. Keeping them in good order saves both time and money. Painted timber needs the most care, requiring a fresh coat at least every two years. Stained timber needs similar treatment but preservative is far quicker and easier to apply. For real ease of maintenance there are conservatories and greenhouses produced from aluminium or plastic-coated metal – both look good and need very little attention. For any glass building to look and work at its best, the glass should be kept clean, so access is an important consideration when initially siting the structure. Cleaning can be carried out with a lightweight, long-handled broom or mop. Never climb on an unsupported surface and always keep a few panes of glass handy in case of breakages. Gutters and downpipes should be checked and cleared yearly. Summerhouses and gazebos need checking, particularly the roofs; a missing tile, slate or

shingle lets in moisture which can quickly affect the rest of the building. If possible, stand the building just off any wall, to provide access and prevent damp, and try and get a good view of the roof so that you can check for any faults.

STRUCTURES

An annual check in autumn will indicate any rotten timbers which should be replaced before the winter storms. Apply preservative after removing climbers, preferably dropping wires and plants together. Check the wires too (use plastic-coated wire where possible for the longest life). If your overheads are made of acrylic or plastic, which can look very elegant if correctly designed, then you have the best of all situations: just a wash to remove any grime.

ABOVE *Timber pergolas or arches should use pressure-treated wood for construction. Support climbers if necessary with neat wires.*

BELOW *Barbecues should be soundly built with ample workspace and built-in storage. Integral seating will be useful and planting will soften it.*

WATER

Too often the thought of a garden pond conjures up images of tangled weeds with a glimpse of brackish water. Many people shy away from pools in the garden because they fear high-maintenance. In fact nothing could be further from the truth; if the feature is built and stocked correctly, then work can be reduced to a minimum. Depth is important – about 45cm (18in) is ideal. A marginal shelf should be provided so that plants that enjoy these conditions can be positioned accordingly. Stock

should include plants, fish and snails, all in proportion to the surface area of water, to achieve a balanced system. Many good garden centres and specialist aquatic companies now sell complete collections of all the livestock and plants needed for a specific size of pool, together with planting baskets, liners, pumps and other equipment.

Always site a pool in an open sunny area, away from overhanging trees. If you follow these basic rules, very little after-care is needed. However, leaves can be a problem. A simple solution is to net the pool with a fine plastic mesh for those few weeks in autumn. Once fall is complete, remove the net and the leaves along with it.

ABOVE *This water feature is straightforward to construct, safe for children and makes an ideal raised bed as shown here (and below).*

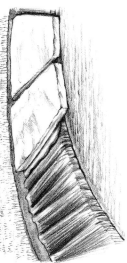

ABOVE *A pool that uses a liner needs a sensible coping to disguise this.*

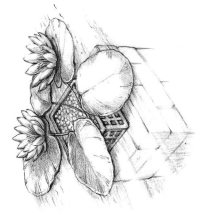

BELOW *Aquatic plants should be positioned in baskets, lined with hessian and filled with soil.*

Soft Landscape

While hard landscape forms the bones of a garden, its counterpart puts flesh on the composition. Whatever the shape, style and content of your outside room, all plants need a healthy growing medium, whether they be planted directly into the ground or in some kind of container or raised bed. We have already discussed the importance of a well-textured, nutritious soil. If this is to be achieved and the garden is to be maintained easily, then good drainage is paramount. In most town gardens this can be brought about by thorough cultivation but in a larger plot land drains may need to be incorporated, these being directed into a soakaway filled with rubble.

Assuming that drainage is adequate, the ground needs to be prepared for planting. If this is done properly, cultivation of the soil need only be carried out every five or six years. Even if there is a framework of existing

plant material, then quite large areas can still be prepared for long-term, virtually maintenance-free borders.

Deep beds need 'double digging' (see illustration), involving removing a trench of soil to a full spade's depth, forking the bottom of the trench over to a similar depth and then working in a layer of compost or other organic material. The next trench is then thrown into the one just prepared. This may seem like hard work, and to do it properly involves considerable effort, but once done it will save a great deal of labour later on.

Never try and dig a whole bed or border in one go and, if you can, use stainless steel tools. These may be more expensive but they last a lifetime and cut through soil like butter. Soil cultivation should also be carried out at the right time of year, preferably in autumn so that freshly turned ground can be broken down by the natural effects of weather during the winter.

In order to maintain the structure of the soil once a deep bed has been prepared, it will be essential not to walk over the surface. The maximum width should be about 1.2 5m (4ft) to allow easy access to plants without damaging the bed. If a border is wider than this, which is unusual in a small town garden, then a stepping-stone path should be incorporated, which may also be useful for easy access to a fence or adjoining wall. In order to prevent compaction by rain, a deep top dressing of finely chopped bark is useful. It will help to retain moisture during dry weather, insulate the soil against cold in winter and spring, vastly reduce the incidence of weed growth and also give a neat and workmanlike finish to the completed border.

ABOVE Remove a trench of soil to one spade's depth, then fork a further spade's depth and work in a layer of compost or other organic material.

BELOW Dig another trench in the same way and use the soil removed from it to fill in the previous trench.

ABOVE Good soil preparation and the provision of adequate nutrients are essential especially in town. Raised beds bring plants to easy working height.

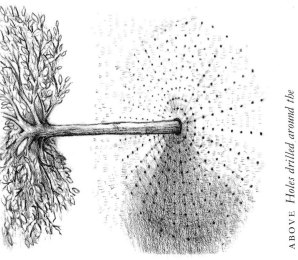

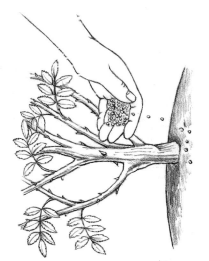

ABOVE Holes drilled around the base of a tree allow slow release fertilizer to be brushed in.

BELOW AND RIGHT Established plants can be fed in pellet form during spring, or (below) with liquid feed in summer.

FEEDING YOUR PLANTS

Garden plants become quickly tired if not fed regularly. Fertilizers come in two forms – organic (natural) and inorganic (artificial). Both are acceptable for garden use. While it could be difficult to incorporate barrows full of rotted manure in the centre of the city, there are a number of excellent organic nutrients available. Most of these can be used in liquid form, either mixed in a watering can and applied by hand or applied through an automatic irrigation system (see page 136). Most inorganic fertilizers are pelleted and can either be carefully sprinkled between plants by hand or diluted and applied in a hand-held spray.

Times of application vary but it is essential to incorporate a slow-release fertilizer such as bonemeal when planting anything in the garden. Once plants are established, nutrients in pellet form should be applied in spring and liquid types during the summer months.

Lawns need their own treatment and this can be a combined application of fertilizer and weedkiller during the spring, with a second feed during autumn to take the sward through the winter. There are a number of wheeled spreaders that make lawn treatments very simple to apply.

Trees and hedges often get overlooked. Both take a great deal of food and water from the ground and only need a little attention. Always incorporate a slow-release fertilizer when planting and then feed at least once a year during growth. For hedges fertilizer can be

incorporated when treating the other border areas, but with a tree set in a lawn the approach is slightly different. For this you will need to drill holes around the tree about 60cm (2ft) apart and 23cm (9in) deep over the area covered by the branches. Into this you can brush a slow-release fertilizer and top up with soil. This is best done in spring.

One last problem concerns acid-loving plants, such as rhododendrons, azaleas, camellias and pieris. For this it is vital to ensure that the soil maintains its acidity; the application of Sequestrene early in the growing season will maintain vigour and prevent leaves turning yellow, a sure sign of alkaline conditions. Peat can also be used, but remember that, although this will increase acidity and improve soil condition, it is not a fertilizer in its own right.

Pruning

One word that, more than any other, causes confusion to many gardeners is pruning. This is largely because of misrepresentation by both professionals and amateurs. The process is actually very simple — not as mysterious as you may have been led to believe.. This relatively straightforward operation is one of the most useful jobs in the garden.

If you look at a natural situation, with plants growing wild, you will see that, although specimens reach large and often unwieldy proportions, they are more often than not a tangled mass of straggly growth. In part this is due to a lack of available plant food, but of more significance is the basic need for each individual to fight for light and air. This means that plants are drawn upwards, leaving bare stems below. Such plants would do little to enhance a domestic garden situation. By becoming entwined, the centre of the plant also suffers, with resulting die-back and an increased chance for disease to take hold.

The whole purpose of pruning is therefore threefold. The first need is to keep a plant or shrub within reasonable bounds; the smaller a garden the more important this is. Urban gardens are often tiny, so as well as choosing plant material wisely, with a view to its eventual size, it will be important in some cases to start pruning from an early age to produce the final size and shape you want. Obviously a well-thought-out plan with plants of modest eventual size will do much to reduce pruning, but it would be a pity altogether to eliminate other species of real merit just because their eventual size was too large.

The second reason is one of general health. If we let plants run their natural course, they become misshapen and over-competitive. If pruned back to remove the longer growths and those stems that turn into the middle of the plant, the need for competition is done away with, light and air penetrates to all parts and the resulting plants are by far the better for it. At the same time any weak, damaged or diseased wood is disposed of and this, too, will increase vigour and productivity, in terms of both fruit and flower.

A final direct result of all this is the simple fact that by pruning

When to prune

EARLY SPRING

SHRUBS: clematis — summer flowering
ROSES: hybrid tea and floribunda (also in November)
TREES: most summer-flowering deciduous trees

SPRING

SHRUBS: hydrangea, buddleia, hypericum, cytisus (broom), ribes (flowering currant), cornus (dogwood), salix (willows), *Hypericum calycinum*, vinca, ericas

ROSES: climbing roses
HERBACEOUS: all late-flowering
HEDGES: laurel, bay, *Aucuba japonica*, elaeagnus

LATE SPRING

SHRUBS: clematis — spring-flowering
TREES: all broad-leaved evergreens

LATE SUMMER

SHRUBS: *philadelphus viburnum*
TREES: all conifers

MIDSUMMER AND EARLY AUTUMN

HEDGES: (need two clips) yew, box, beech, rosemary, hornbeam, escallonia, pyracantha

AUTUMN

ROSES: hybrid tea and floribunda (see Spring)
HERBACEOUS: all early-flowering
TREES: some summer-flowering deciduous

you are shortening the stems. All stems have buds along their length; so those below the cut are going to shoot, thus producing bushy growth low down. This means that a sensibly pruned plant will be vigorous, healthy and well shaped, with plenty of shoots coming from the bottom. Such a bushy specimen will in the majority of cases be far better and healthier than one left alone. Different types of plants are pruned in slightly different ways.

SHRUBS

As a general rule select shrubs that have a good shape. Minor trimming can take place when planting, but this should only involve the removal of any damaged wood. Reject any plants that are misshapen or

unbalanced. The time of pruning depends on when the shrub flowers and whether it is on new or old growth. Hydrangeas, buddleias and hypericum all flower during late summer, on wood produced during that growing season. Such plants should therefore be pruned early in the year just as they are starting to move. Cut them back to within two or three buds of the previous year's growth.

The second main group are those shrubs that flower during the spring, including cytisus (broom), ribes (flowering currant) and forsythia. These and plants like them should be pruned after flowering to allow ample time for new wood to develop for the coming year. Cut back as many shoots that have flowered as possible, at the same

time removing any dead or damaged branches. Taller deciduous shrubs, such as philadelphus or viburnum which can be useful in a town garden to soften the lines of the walls and fences, can simply be thinned out after flowering, with a more severe pruning when plants become elderly.

Another group are those shrubs grown for the interest of their stems during winter. Cornus (dogwood) and some of the smaller salix (willows) are typical of these, and because they can be pruned hard they can be safely grown in a relatively small garden. As the colour is shown best on the new wood, they should be cut back to within two or three buds of the old wood in March, thus allowing ample time for new stems to develop.

Shrubs which flower in spring should be pruned after flowering. Cut back as many as possible of the shoots which have flowered.

When pruning make a sharp, oblique cut no more than 12mm ($\frac{1}{2}$in) above the bud, preferably an outward-facing one.

Shrubs flowering in late summer should be pruned early in year to within two or three buds of previous year's growth.

Ground-covering plants should remain just that: many varieties get leggy unless clipped over with a pair of shears in spring. Such treatment keeps plants such as *Hypericum calycinum*, vinca and erica as tight, closely knit clumps, ideal for the production of flower and for keeping maintenance to an absolute minimum.

Clematis are particularly useful in town gardens for their

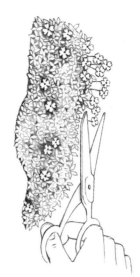

ABOVE Smaller lower growing plants can be more carefully trimmed with scissors. Helianthemum falls into this category: carefully remove dead blooms and towards the end of July, cut out long straggly stems.

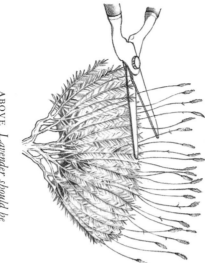

ABOVE Lavender should be regularly clipped after flowering each year: use the spent blooms for lavender bags. The plants can be trimmed back in April but avoid cutting into the old wood.

wealth of bloom and their tolerance of shade. In fact, most clematis flowers retain colour far better in shade than sun. There is, however, always a degree of confusion over the pruning of different types. They are divided into three classifications — those that flower in early spring, those producing bloom in mid-summer and late-blooming varieties. Spring-flowering clematis include *C. montana*, *C. alpina* and *C. macropetala*. These can be left virtually untouched, and they will spread over a considerable distance. If they become too large they can then be pruned back after flowering, removing the stems that have borne flowers and spreading the remainder out to produce flowers the following year. If dramatic pruning is required, they can be cut back hard in the spring, but remember that by doing this you will lose bloom for the coming year. The large-flowered varieties such as 'Nellie Moser' and 'The President' together with the large summer-flowering types including 'Ville de Lyon' and C. ×*jackmanii* should be pruned in the early part of the year, February being ideal. They should be cut back hard to a strong pair of buds approximately 30cm (12in) above the ground. The late-flowering species such as C. *tangutica* and C. *viticella* should also be pruned at this time, that is in the early part of the year. However, as they have rather longer to produce new wood on which to flower, they are cut back even harder to a strong pair of buds just above ground level.

TRAINING SHRUBS

Pruning shrubs and climbers promotes vigour and keeps plants within manageable proportions.

Training shrubs is rather different and allows a plant to be moulded to a particular shape or fill a specific situation.

Some species are more adaptable than others and many enjoy the support provided by a

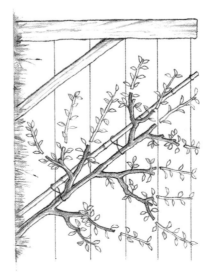

wall, even though they are not climbers in their own right. As an example, pyracantha is excellent, a fast growing, evergreen shrub with the benefit of orange or yellow berries in autumn and throughout the winter. Left to its own devices it forms a sprawling, fairly open shrub but given the backing of a wall and clipped after flowering it can be trained into any number of architectural patterns.

Another good choice would be chaenomeles, or flowering quince. The blossom comes early in the year, but again, the plant needs trimming and training during the summer. Plant it with *Euonymus radicans* 'Silver Queen' which also enjoys the backing of a wall and which will provide a fascinating contrast.

ROSES

Many roses, especially the hybrid tea and floribunda types, are ideal for an urban garden. Both of these should be pruned hard in spring to an outward-facing bud, thus keeping the centre of the plant open and preventing a tangle of shoots in the middle. Hybrid teas should be cut back to 4–6 buds from the base and floribundas slightly less hard, to 6–8 buds. March is really the latest this can be carried out, although you should think of shortening long stems that might be damaged by strong winter winds during the previous November. Climbing and rambling roses should only be lightly pruned if they get too large. Dead wood, together with any very old or weakened stems, can be removed in the spring. Deadheading of all rose types is beneficial during the flowering season, and prolongs the display.

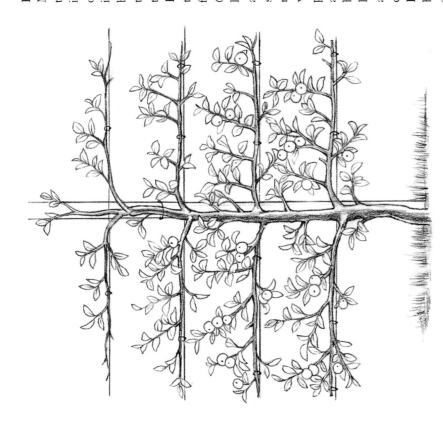

Train espalier fruit bushes on horizontal wires. The main stem should be cut just above three good buds. In the first season tie the top shoot vertically, the others at 45°. In the second winter bring these shoots down to the lowest horizontal wire and cut back to a third their length. Prune the vertical shoot to the next wire up and repeat the whole operation the following season.

Prune roses moderately, cutting diagonally to an outward-facing bud. Cut hybrid teas (above) slightly harder than floribundas (right).

HERBACEOUS PLANTS

We have seen that herbaceous plants (hardy perennials) are an integral part of any scheme, having the benefit of rapid growth and consequent low maintenance. To keep them at their best they should be divided every three or four years, because the best blooms are usually produced on newer wood. As a general rule, lift, divide and replant the early-flowering varieties in autumn and the later-flowering subjects in the spring. The most vigorous and healthy part of a herbaceous plant is around the perimeter and it is this section that should be divided and replanted. The largely dead central section can be discarded. Some plants, of which heuchera is a good example, grow progressively further out of the ground each year. This results in a loss of flowering potential. Divide these in exactly the same way, and replant them at ground level.

Many gardening books claim that hardy perennials demand

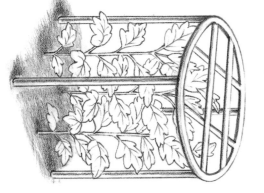

ABOVE Taller hardy perennials need support with a wire frame.

the most maintenance in the garden, and there is no doubt that a traditional herbaceous border needs regular feeding, staking and tying. However, a mixed shrub border with herbaceous plants to 'lift' the composition with added colour and texture is an altogether different matter. The secret here, as we have seen earlier, is to allow the shrubs to support the perennials. The choice of perennials should be angled towards newer varieties that are bred somewhat shorter and are therefore more robust than their predecessors. If a plant does need staking, and some are well

ABOVE This is a subtle piece of design. The timber fence and gate echo the weatherboard building. The trimmed hedge forms an attractive arch.

worth the small amount of work required, then it will be best to buy prefabricated frames through which plants can grow. These are usually made from galvanized or plastic-coated wire so as to preclude maintenance. They can be positioned in spring and removed in autumn when the plants die down.

HEDGES

The choice of hedge for a low-maintenance town garden is important. Some, such as privet (*Ligustrum*) and *Lonicera nitida*, are really not suitable, since they need attention throughout the year to keep them in check. Others that need less clipping can be very useful, either being trained into a formal pattern or allowed to grow naturally into a loose but effective barrier. The choice should depend on the space available.

Many hedges need two trims a year – a main cut in mid-summer, about July or August, and a final trim in the early autumn to remove growth put on since the summer. Varieties that need this include yew (*Taxus baccata*), box (*Buxus*), beech (*Fagus*) and hornbeam (*Carpinus*), many of the conifers including lawsoniana, and some of the flowering hedges such as escallonia, pyracantha and rosemary. Others, and these are obviously ideal, need a single cut. Examples include laurel (*Prunus laurocerasus*), bay (*Laurus nobilis*), *Aucuba japonica* and elaeagnus. Most of these form a loose but dense hedge and are better clipped with secateurs than a pair of shears.

All too often one sees hedges that are wider at the top than the bottom. This inevitably means that the lower sections are bare and straggly because they are starved of light, air and moisture. Always clip a hedge in a wedge shape so that it tapers gently towards the top, it looks neat and stays dense right down to the ground.

Pruning may sound like a tedious task, but broken down into its basic components, it is really very simple indeed. If you plant the garden correctly, check which of the soft landscape components need attention at what time of year, and carry the work out on a regular basis, then work will be kept to a minimum. It would be fair to say that all the pruning in a small town garden measuring 8m (25ft) square could take as little as six hours per year – a small allocation of time to keep your outside room looking its best.

TREES

Because of their size and seeming indestructability, trees often get little or no maintenance, often shortening their life span considerably.

Newly planted trees need regular checking and feeding to see that they get the best start in life. Any young tree should be securely staked with a stout post and two rubber ties that can be slackened off as the stem expands. The habit of using a bamboo cane and wire to secure a tree is a bad one, as the roots get little chance to establish because of constant buffeting by the wind. Wire, with or without a firm stake, should never be used because it cuts into the growing tissue, which will allow the beginnings of disease and ultimately even sever the trunk.

Care of a mature tree means an annual check to see if any branches need attention. Dead and diseased timber should be cut out and, if these are large or high above the ground, it will be well worth employing a skilled tree surgeon to carry out the work for you. The fee may seem expensive but it will be money well spent, particularly when accidents can and do happen with untrained personnel. This may be an ideal opportunity to thin the tree out and allow more light and air into the garden. However, make sure that you are not opening the sight-line to a neighbour's window or an unwanted view. Lower and lighter branches can be more easily removed, but always rope the branch in question to a strong limb above and do the job in two sections, removing the main length first and neatly

cleaning up the remaining stub close to the main trunk. Pruning a tree will increase its vigour but unless it is done properly, by removing limbs rather than the ends of branches, there is little point in the operation.

Some trees, including many cherries and standard weeping trees, are grafted onto a particular root-stock. This is normally visible as a union just above ground level or at the top of the stem. This lower stock can be more vigorous than that of the grafted tree above and there may be a tendency for suckers to appear below the graft. These should be removed as soon as possible. Should a tree be felled and a stump remain, it is advisable to remove this altogether. A rotten stump is prone to a number of diseases and these can easily be transferred to other plant material in the garden. Stumps flush with the surface can be ground out or, it left longer, roots can be severed and levered out.

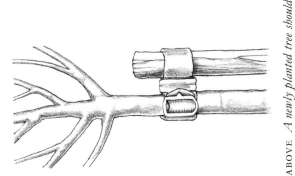

ABOVE *A newly planted tree should be firmly staked and secured.*

Irrigation and incidentals

To keep plants in a vigorous and healthy condition, watering is of paramount importance. Many town gardens have a particular 'microclimate', that is, an individual set of very local weather conditions that do not necessarily conform to those in the adjoining open country. Sometimes this is beneficial, as city gardens can be havens of warmer air with markedly higher temperatures during the winter. On the debit side, pollution can be a problem and so, too, can rainfall. While the latter can fall in quantity, the presence of high walls, adjoining buildings and overhanging eaves can combine to produce a 'rain shadow', which means that the plants in your garden may receive very little moisture.

In very basic terms this will mean you will have to irrigate certain areas copiously to maintain growth. This may mean the provision of an outside

Oscillating sprinklers make irrigation easy.

tap; in very small gardens, regular use of a watering can in the morning and evening may well be all that is needed. The bigger the plot, however, the more difficult this is and some form of automatic system will almost certainly be necessary. When you think that a thickly planted border of 2m (6ft) square can require up to 10 litres (17½ pints) of water per day during a hot summer, then the scale of the problem is clear.

A trip to any garden centre will quickly produce a wealth of watering gadgets from lengths of perforated hose to complicated computer systems. The point is to find which is best for you. In basic terms it all depends on area and cash available. For a very small garden a static sprinkler that takes the form of a circular spray set on a ground spike is ideal. This can either cover the whole garden or be moved from bed to bed. The distance of the spray can be determined to some degree by turning the tap up or down. Rotary sprinklers are a stage up from this, covering a larger area, while oscillating types are the best for altogether bigger gardens.

Irrigation can also be obtained by perforated hoses that can be laid through a border and kept in place. More complicated automatic irrigation systems can be tailored to a specific garden, balcony or penthouse terrace. Some of these can be bought in kit form and come complete with a timer that can be programmed and cuts off at a set time. The most complicated are installed by specialist companies, can be completely concealed and are equipped with 'pop-up' irrigation heads that are managed by a small computer. They are safe, robust and can be programmed and left to operate while you are away.

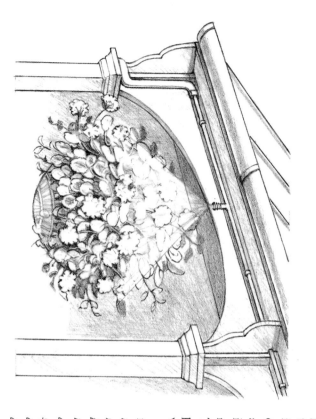

LEFT *Hanging baskets can be tedious and difficult to water. To make the job easier, fit an automatic irrigation line. This can be fixed to the underside of eaves with nozzles above each basket. These can be of a spray or drip kind and they can be activated manually or wired into an automatic system.*

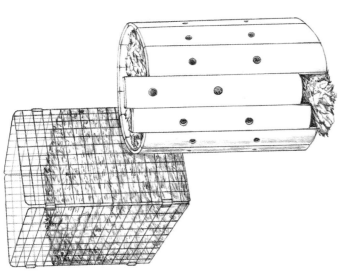

INCIDENTALS

Barbecues are fine in the summer but look depressing in the winter. If you have a portable give it a good clean and store it away in the dry. Built-in barbecues can have the metal cooking grids removed for cleaning and storage and the feature makes an excellent surface for pots of winter-flowering shrubs and bulbs – providing instant colour at a dull time of the year. Sandpits should be covered with a stout wooden top and play equipment checked for safety and lubrication. If you have a surface of chipped bark around swings and slides, then top this up.

Portable wooden furniture should be stored in winter and lightly oiled, but a better alternative might be a well-designed plastic set that can stand out all year round and save valuable space, always at a premium in town. Tools and equipment need an annual winter check and power tools should be serviced for maximum efficiency next season.

Compost bins in a town garden are considered by many to be a waste of time and bags full of invaluable organic matter are regularly put out for the dustmen. Urban soil is often tired and needs as much goodness putting back as possible. Compost is by far the best solution, improving soil texture and replacing nutrients. A small compost bin, tucked away in a corner, can be a real asset, and easier to fill than countless plastic bags. Some ventilation is essential, and the top should be partially open at all times to let in air.

RIGHT *No matter what the size of your garden, a compost bin is an invaluable addition. Leaves, grass cuttings, dead flowers and so on can be stored to provide valuable compost. Decay can be speeded up by mixing in an accelerator. Wire cages provide less protection than plastic bins and are best suited to leaf mould. The bin slats lift up, allowing easy access to rotten compost at the bottom. Being more compact, they are especially suitable for small gardens.*

BELOW *This outside room combines low-maintenance features such as the flooring and plastic table-cloth to provide an informal eating area.*

Plant Directory

Key   cvs – cultivars   sp – species   *– evergreen

COMMON NAME	HEIGHT	COMMENTS
TREES AND SHRUBS FOR SCREENING		
*Arundinaria — Bamboo	3 to 4.5m (10 to 15ft)	Spreading growth
*Betula — Birch	3.6 to 15m (12 to 50ft)	Upright growth; attractive bark
*Berberis × stenophylla — Barberry	2.1 to 2.7m (7 to 9ft)	Spreading growth; yellow flowers in spring
*Cryptomeria japonica 'Elegans' — Japanese Cedar	7.6 to 12m (25 to 40ft)	Spreading growth
*× Cupressocyparis leylandii — Leyland Cypress	15 to 27m (50 to 90ft)	Spreading growth; extremely fast grower
*Cupressus macrocarpa 'Lutea' — Golden Monterey Cypress	7.6 to 12m (25 to 40ft)	Spreading growth
*Elaeagnus × ebbingei	1.5 to 2.1m (5 to 7ft)	Spreading growth
*Escallonia cvs	1.2 to 3m (4 to 10ft)	Spreading growth; pink, red or white flowers
Eucalyptus — Gum	12 to 27m (40 to 90ft)	Upright growth; attractive bark
Ligustrum — Privet	2.1 to 3.3m (7 to 11ft)	Spreading growth
Polygonum baldschuanicum — Russian Vine	4.5 to 9m (15 to 30ft)	Climber; vigorous; white flowers
Prunus avium — Gean, Wild Cherry	7.6 to 13.7m (25 to 45ft)	Spreading growth; white flowers
Prunus cerasifera 'Pissardii' — Purple Leaved Plum	4.5 to 7.6m (15 to 25ft)	Spreading growth; young foliage dark red turning purple
*Prunus laurocerasus — Common Laurel, Cherry Laurel	3 to 5.4m (10 to 18ft)	Spreading growth
*Pyracantha — Firethorn	2.7 to 4.8m (9 to 16ft)	Spreading growth; white flowers; orange berries; thorns
Rosa 'Fruhlingsgold'	1.8 to 3.6m (6 to 12ft)	Spreading growth; fragrant pale yellow single flowers
Sorbus aria 'Lutescens' — Whitebeam	6 to 12m (20 to 40ft)	Upright growth; white felt on undersides of leaves
TREES AND SHRUBS FOR DRY, SUNNY POSITIONS		
Artemisia abrotanum — Southernwood, Lad's Love	60cm to 1.2m (2 to 4ft)	Spreading growth; aromatic, silver foliage
*Berberis — Barberry	45cm to 1.9m (1½ to 6ft)	Spreading growth; yellow and orange flowers; red or purple berries
Buddleia cvs — Butterfly Bush	1.8 to 3m (6 to 10ft)	Spreading growth; flowers of various colours attract butterflies
*Buxus sempervirens — Box	1 to 2.4m (3 to 8ft)	Spreading growth; slow growing
Caryopteris × clandonensis cvs — Blue Spiraea	45 to 75cm (1½ to 2½ft)	Spreading growth; blue flowers late in the season; tolerates chalk
Ceratostigma willmottianum — Hardy Plumbago	38 to 60cm (15in to 2ft)	Spreading growth; blue flowers
Chaenomeles speciosa cvs — Flowering Quince	2.1 to 4.5m (7 to 15ft)	Spreading growth; early flowers in shades of red, pink and white
*Cistus — Sun Rose	15cm to 1.8m (6in to 6ft)	Spreading growth; pink or white flowers; tolerates chalk
*Convolvulus cneorum	45 to 60cm (1½ to 2ft)	Spreading growth; silver foliage; white flowers
Cotinus coggygria — Smoke Bush	2.7 to 4.5m (9 to 15ft)	Spreading growth; autumn colour; 'foamy' flower heads
Cytisus cvs — Broom	45cm to 1.8m (1½ to 6ft)	Spreading growth; flowers white or shades of yellow and red; tolerates lime
*Erica cvs — Heather	15cm to 2.4m (6in to 8ft)	Spreading and upright growth; colour and form according to species and variety
*Euonymus cvs	45cm to 2.4m (1½ to 8ft)	Spreading growth; choose evergreen forms with variegated foliage
Fuchsia cvs	1 to 2.1m (3 to 7ft)	Spreading growth; flower colour varies with cv
Genista hispanica — Spanish Gorse	30 to 60cm (1 to 2ft)	Spreading growth; mass of yellow flowers
Hedysarum	1 to 2.4m (3 to 8ft)	Spreading growth; flower colour varies with sp
Hibiscus cvs — Rose Mallow	2.1 to 4.2m (7 to 14ft)	Upright growth; late flowers in shades of pink, violet and white
*Hypericum cvs	15cm to 1.2m (6in to 4ft)	Spreading growth; yellow flowers
*Lavandula cvs — Lavender	45cm to 1m (1½ to 3ft)	Spreading growth; aromatic grey foliage; pink or blue flowers
Lavatera olbia — Tree Mallow	1.5 to 2.4m (5 to 8ft)	Spreading growth; soft grey foliage; pink flowers
Lupinus arboreus — Tree Lupin	1.2 to 2.1m (4 to 7ft)	Spreading growth; yellow flowers
Lycium barbarum — Duke of Argyll's Tea Tree	1.5 to 2.1m (5 to 7ft)	Spreading growth; purple flowers; spines
*Olearia — Daisy Bush	1 to 1.5m (3 to 5ft)	Spreading growth; white daisy flowers

	COMMON NAME	HEIGHT	COMMENTS
Potentilla fruticosa cvs	Shrubby Cinquefoil	45cm to 1.5m (15in to 5ft)	Spreading growth; flowers usually yellow
Robina pseudoacacia	False Acacia Tree	9 to 15m (30 to 50ft)	Upright growth; white flowers
Rosa cvs	Rose	Variable	Wide range of form and flower colour; heps
Rosmarinus	Rosemary	15cm to 1.8m (6in to 6ft)	Spreading and upright growth; aromatic foliage
Santolina chamaecyparissus syn. *S. Incana*	Lavender Cotton	38cm to 1m (15in to 3ft)	Spreading growth; silver foliage
Senecio 'Sunshine'		1 to 1.5m (3 to 5ft)	Spreading growth; grey foliage; yellow flowers
Spartium junceum	Spanish Broom	1.8 to 2.4m (6 to 8ft)	Spreading growth; yellow flowers
Tamarix tetrandra	Tamarisk	2.4 to 3.6m (8 to 12ft)	Spreading growth; small pink flowers
Ulex europaeus	Gorse	1.2 to 2.4m (4 to 8ft)	Spreading growth; yellow flowers
Vinca	Periwinkle	10 to 15cm (4 to 6in)	Spreading growth; mauve or white flowers; creeping habit
Yucca		1.5 to 3m (5 to 10ft)	Upright growth; tall cream flower spike

TREES AND SHRUBS FOR SHADY POSITIONS

	COMMON NAME	HEIGHT	COMMENTS
Arundinaria	Bamboo	3 to 4.5m (10 to 15ft)	Spreading growth
Aucuba japonica cvs	Spotted Laurel	1.5 to 2.7m (5 to 9ft)	Spreading growth
Berberis	Barberry	45cm to 1.8m (1½ to 6ft)	Spreading growth; yellow or orange flowers; red or purple fruit
Camellia cvs		1.5 to 2.4m (5 to 8ft)	Spreading growth; flowers white or shades of pink, varied in form; lime-free soil
Chaenomeles speciosa cvs	Flowering Quince	2.1 to 4.5m (7 to 15ft)	Spreading growth; early flowers in shades of pink, red or white
Clethra alnifolia	Sweet Pepper Bush	1.5 to 2.7m (5 to 9ft)	Spreading growth; white fragrant flowers
Cornus alba 'Sibirica'	Westonbirt Dogwood	1.2 to 2.4m (4 to 8ft)	Spreading growth; bright red winter stems
Corylopsis	Winter Hazel	1 to 4.5m (3 to 15ft)	Spreading growth; pale yellow, fragrant flowers appear before foliage
Cotoneaster horizontalis		30 to 38cm (12 to 15in)	Spreading growth; red berries
Danae racemosa	Alexandrian Laurel	60cm to 1m (2 to 3ft)	Spreading growth
Daphne mezereum	Mezereon	1.5 to 2.9m (5 to 9ft)	Spreading growth; pink flowers; poisonous fruits
Deutzia cvs		1.2 to 2.1m (4 to 7ft)	Spreading growth; pink or white flowers
Disanthus cercidifolius		2.1 to 4.5m (7 to 15ft)	Spreading growth; autumn colour
Elaeagnus		1.2 to 2.7m (6 to 9ft)	Spreading growth
Enkianthus campanulatus		2.1 to 2.7m (7 to 9ft)	Spreading growth; lime-free soil
Euonymus alata	Spindle Berry	2.1 to 2.7m (7 to 9ft)	Spreading growth; autumn colour
Fatsia japonica	Fig Leaf Palm	1.2 to 2.1m (4 to 7ft)	Spreading growth; white flowers; large lobed leaves
Gaultheria shallon		1.5 to 2.1m (5 to 7ft)	Spreading growth; pale pink flowers; purple fruits
Hedera cvs	Ivy	4.5 to 12m (15 to 40ft)	Climber; many cvs have variegated foliage
Hydrangea		60cm to 2.7m (2 to 9ft)	Spreading growth; pink or blue flowers according to soil
Hypericum calycinum	Rose of Sharon	15 to 23cm (6 to 9in)	Spreading growth; vigorous ground coverer; yellow flowers
Leucothoe fontanesiana		1 to 1.8m (3 to 6ft)	Spreading growth; ground coverer for lime-free soils; white flowers
Mahonia cvs		45cm to 1.5m (1½ to 5ft)	Spreading growth; yellow flowers in winter and early spring
Pachysandra terminalis		15 to 23cm (6 to 9in)	Spreading growth
Pieris cvs	Lily-of-the-valley Tree	1.8 to 6m (6 to 20ft)	Spreading growth; several cvs have young red foliage
Pyracantha	Firethorn	2.7 to 4.8m (9 to 16ft)	Spreading growth; white flowers; orange berries
Rhododendron cvs		30cm to 6m (1 to 20ft)	Spreading and upright growth; lime-free soil
Rubus		1 to 2.7m (3 to 9ft)	Spreading growth; ornamental brambles
Sarcococca	Christmas Box	38 to 60cm (15in to 2ft)	Spreading growth
Skimmia cvs		1 to 1.5m (3 to 5ft)	Spreading growth; plant male and female plants for red berries
Symphoricarpos	Snowberry	1.2 to 1.8m (4 to 6ft)	Spreading growth; white or pink berries
Vaccinium corymbosum	High-bush Blueberry	1.5 to 1.8m (5 to 6ft)	Spreading growth; lime-free soil; edible berries

TREES AND SHRUBS RESISTANT TO POLLUTION

	COMMON NAME	HEIGHT	COMMENTS
Acer cvs	Maple	1.2 to 15m (4 to 50ft)	Spreading and upright growth; autumn colour
Berberis (deciduous kinds)	Barberry	45cm to 1.8m (1½ to 6ft)	Spreading growth; yellow or orange flowers; red or purple berries
Betula	Birch	3.6 to 4.5m (12 to 15ft)	Spreading and upright growth; attractive bark
Buddleia cvs	Butterfly Bush	1.8 to 3m (6 to 10ft)	Spreading growth; flowers attract butterflies
Chaenomeles speciosa cvs	Flowering Quince	2.1 to 4.5m (7 to 15ft)	Spreading growth; early flowers in shades of pink, red or white
Cotoneaster (deciduous kinds)		45cm to 2.4m (1½in to 8ft)	Spreading growth; red berries
Crataegus		4.5 to 7.6m (15 to 25ft)	Haws and autumn colour
Daphne mezereum	Mezereon	1.5 to 2.4m (5 to 8ft)	Spreading growth; pink flowers, poisonous fruits
Deutzia cvs		1.2 to 2.1m (4 to 7ft)	Spreading growth; pink or white flowers
Euonymus fortunei var. radicans		15 to 30cm (6 to 12in)	Spreading growth; will trail or climb
Fatsia japonica	Fig-leaf Palm	1.2 to 2.1m (4 to 7ft)	Spreading growth; white flowers; large, lobed leaves
Forsythia		2.1 to 4.5m (7 to 15ft)	Spreading growth; yellow flowers
Hebe brachysiphon		1.2 to 1.5m (4 to 5ft)	Spreading growth; white flowers
Hedera cvs	Ivy	4.5 to 12m (15 to 40ft)	Climber; self-clinging; autumn colour
Hibiscus cvs	Rose Mallow	2.1 to 4.2m (7 to 14ft)	Upright growth; late flowers in shades of pink, violet and white
Hypericum cvs		15cm to 1.2m (6in to 4ft)	Spreading growth; yellow flowers
Jasminum nudiflorum	Winter Jasmine	2.4 to 4.2m (8 to 14ft)	Climber; yellow winter flowers
Kerria japonica 'Pleniflora'	Jew's Mallow	1.2 to 1.8m (4 to 6ft)	Spreading growth; green stems; yellow flowers
Laburnum × watereri 'Vossii'	Golden Chain Tree	3.6 to 6m (12 to 20ft)	Upright growth; clusters of yellow flowers
Ligustrum	Privet	2.1 to 3.3m (7 to 11ft)	Spreading growth
Mahonia cvs		45cm to 1.5m (1½ to 15ft)	Spreading growth; yellow flowers in winter and early spring
Malus cvs	Crab Apple	4.5 to 7.6m (15 to 25ft)	Spreading growth; spring blossom; autumn fruit
Olearia × haastii	Daisy Bush	1.2 to 1.8m (4 to 6ft)	Spreading growth; white flowers
Parthenocissus quinquefolia	Virginia Creeper	3.6 to 12m (12 to 40ft)	Climber; autumn colour
Pernettya	Prickly Heath	60cm to 1.5m (2 to 5ft)	Spreading growth; white flowers; brilliant berries
Philadelphus cvs	Mock Orange	1.8 to 4.5m (6 to 15ft)	Spreading growth; white fragrant flowers
Prunus cvs	Flowering Cherries	2.7 to 7.6m (9 to 25ft)	Spreading and upright growth; pink or white blossom
Pyracantha	Firethorn	2.7 to 4.8m (9 to 16ft)	Spreading growth; white flowers; orange berries
Rhus typhina	Stag's Horn Sumach	2.4 to 4.5m (8 to 15ft)	Spreading growth; autumn colour
Ribes sanguineum	Flowering Currant	1.8 to 2.4m (5 to 8ft)	Upright growth; pink flowers
Rosa cvs	Rose	45cm to 3m (1½ to 10ft)	Wide range of form and flower
Senecio 'Sunshine'		1 to 1.5m (3 to 5ft)*	Spreading growth; grey foliage; yellow flowers; suitable for seaside
Sorbus		7.5cm to 7.6m (2½ to 25ft)	Upright growth
Spiraea cvs		45cm to 1.2m (1½ to 4ft)	Spreading growth; graceful flowering shrubs
Syringa cvs	Lilac	45cm to 3m (1½ to 10ft)	Spreading and upright growth; flowers in shades of pink, mauve and white
Viburnum		1.2 to 2.1m (4 to 7ft)	Varied genus; many have white flowers followed by berries
*Vinca	Periwinkle	10 to 15cm (4 to 6in)	Spreading growth; mauve or white flowers; creeping
Weigela		1.5 to 2.1m (5 to 7ft)	Spreading growth; pink, white or yellow flowers
*Yucca		1.8 to 3m (6 to 10ft)	Spreading growth; tall cream flower spike; suitable for seaside

GROUND COVER PLANTS

	COMMON NAME	HEIGHT	COMMENTS
Ajuga reptans 'Multicolor'	Bugle		Invasive growth; likes dense shade; colourful variegated foliage
Alchemilla mollis	Lady's Mantle		Spreading growth; likes an open situation; small sulphur-yellow flowers
Anaphalis	Pearl Everlasting		Spreading growth; silver foliage; white flowers
Anemone × hybrida	Japanese Anemone		Spreading growth; pink flowers
Artemisia			Likes an open situation; silver foliage

	COMMON NAME	HEIGHT	COMMENTS
Aruncus dioicus	Goat's Beard	Upright growth	white plume-like flowers
Astilbe cvs	False Goat's Beard	Upright growth	plume-like flower spikes in red, pink and white
*Bergenia cvs	Elephant's Ears	Spreading growth	likes dense shade; early pink flowers
Calluna cvs	Scottish Ling	Spreading growth	likes an open situation; many cvs of varied foliage and flower colour
Campanula portenschlagiana	Bellflower	Invasive growth	blue-mauve flowers
Centaurea dealbata	Knapwood	Likes an open situation	pink flowers
Cerastium tomentosum	Snow-in-summer	Spreading growth	likes an open situation; silver foliage; white flowers
Cistus × pulverulentus		Spreading growth	bright pink flowers
Convallaria majalis	Lily-of-the-valley	Invasive growth	likes dense shade; white fragrant flowers
Cornus canadensis	Creeping Dogwood	Invasive growth	likes dense shade; white flowers; red fruits
*Cotoneaster 'Skogholm'		Spreading habit	likes dense shade; red berries
Cyclamen hederifolium		Invasive growth	likes dense shade; marbled foliage; pink flowers
*Daboecia cantabrica cvs	St Daboec's Heath	Likes an open situation	pink flowers; lime-free soil
Dicentra formosa subsp. *oregona*		Invasive growth	pale yellow flowers
Dryopteris		Spreading growth	likes dense shade; easy-to-grow ferns
Epimedium	Barrenwort	Invasive growth	likes dense shade; attractive flowers; decorative foliage
*Erica cvs	Heather	Spreading growth	likes an open situation; flowers and foliage vary with sp and cv
*Euonymus fortunei var. radicans		Spreading growth	likes an open situation
Euphorbia amygdaloides subsp. *robbiae*	Spurge	Invasive growth	likes dense shade; sulphur-yellow flowers
*Festuca glauca	Blue Grass	Invasive growth	likes an open situation
Galium odoratum	Woodruff	Invasive growth	likes dense shade; fragrant grey foliage
*Gaultheria procumbens	Checkerberry	Invasive growth	likes dense shade; bright red fruits in winter
*Gaultheria shallon		Spreading growth	likes dense shade; pale pink flowers; purple fruits
Geranium	Crane's Bill	Spreading growth	likes open situation or dense shade; flowers pink or mauve
Genista hispanica	Spanish Gorse	Spreading growth	likes an open situation; yellow flowers
*Hebe pinguifolia 'Pagei'	Shrubby Speedwell	Spreading growth	green-grey foliage; white flowers
*Hedera cvs	Ivy	Invasive growth	likes dense shade; many cvs have variegated foliage
*Helianthemum cvs	Rock Rose	Spreading growth	likes an open situation; wide range of flower colours
*Helleborus	Hellebore	Likes dense shade	fine foliage; greenish flowers
*Hosta cvs	Plantain Lily	Likes dense shade	wide range of foliage colour
Hydrangea anomala subsp. *petiolaris*	Climbing Hydrangea	Invasive growth	covers a steep bank as well as it covers a wall
*Hypericum calycinum	Rose of Sharon	Invasive growth	likes dense shade; large yellow flowers
*Lamiastrum galeobdolon	Yellow Dead Nettle	Invasive growth	likes dense shade
*Lavandula cvs	Lavender	Spreading growth	pink or mauve flowers; aromatic foliage
Luzula maxima	Creeping Woodrush	Likes dense shade	grass-like foliage
*Mahonia aquifolium	Oregon Grape	Invasive growth	likes dense shade; early yellow flowers; blue berries
Nepeta mussinii	Catmint	Spreading growth	likes an open situation; grey foliage; mauve flowers
Oxalis magellanica		Invasive growth	likes dense shade
*Pachysandra terminalis		Invasive growth	likes dense shade
Polygonum vaccinifolium		Spreading growth	likes an open situation; pink flowers
Pulmonaria	Lungwort	Invasive growth	
Rodgersia		Likes dense shade	handsome foliage
*Rubus tricolor		Invasive growth	trailing stems; white flowers
Salvia	Sage	Spreading growth	likes an open situation; purple and golden-leaved forms available
Santolina chamaecyparissus syn. *S. incana*	Cotton Lavender	Spreading growth	likes an open situation; silver foliage
*Sarcococca bookerana var. digyna		Spreading growth	white flowers; black berries
Saxifraga	Saxifrage	Invasive growth	large and varied genus
*Senecio 'Sunshine'		Spreading growth	yellow flowers; grey foliage
*Stachys byzantina	Lamb's Ear	Spreading growth	likes an open situation; soft felted foliage
*Symphytum ibericum	Comfrey	Invasive growth	likes dense shade; purple flowers
Tellima grandiflora		Invasive growth	likes dense shade; bronzy foliage
Tiarella cordifolia	Foam Flower	Invasive growth	likes dense shade; cream flower spike
Trachystemon orientalis		Invasive growth	likes dense shade; violet flower spikes
*Vinca minor	Periwinkle	Invasive growth	likes dense shade; mauve flowers
*Viburnum davidii		Spreading growth	plant male and female plants for turquoise berries
Viola labradorica	Violet	Invasive growth	blue flowers

Index

Page numbers in *italic* refer to illustrations.

Acknowledgments

The publisher thanks the following photographers and organizations for their kind permission to reproduce the photographs in this book:

2 Christine Tiberghien; 3 Jerry Harpur/Conran Octopus; 5 above centre Lamontagne; 5 above right Philippe Perdereau; 5 below left Marijke Heuff (Patricia van Roosmalen); 5 below centre Ron Sutherland/Garden Picture Library; 5 below right Marijke Heuff (Mr & Mrs Helsen); 6–7 John Heseltine; 8 Ron Sutherland/Garden Picture Library (designed by Duane Paul Design Team); 9 Marijke Heuff (designer Piet Oudolf); 12 Boys Syndication; 13 John Heseltine; 15 left Lamontagne; 15 right Gary Rogers; 16 Marijke Heuff (Mr & Mrs Poley); 16–17 Marijke Heuff (Sue Du Val); 18 left Eric Crichton (Turn End); 19 Jerry Harpur (Mr & Mrs Brinkworth); 21 Gary Rogers; 24–25 Jerry Harpur (Lady Barborolli); 25 Jerry Harpur (designers Keyes Brothers); 26 Jerry Harpur (Mrs Anthony Crossley); 27 Georges Leveque; 30 Jerry Harpur (designer Tim Du Val); 31 Jerry Tubby/Elizabeth Whiting & Associates; 32 left Elizabeth Whiting & Associates; 32 right Jerry Harpur (designer James Hitchmough); 38–39 Marijke Heuff (Mr & Mrs Adriaanse); 40 Ron Sutherland/Garden Picture Library (designed by Duane Paul Design Team); 42 Andrew Lawson; 44 Jerry Harpur (designer James Hitchmough); 45 right Jerry Harpur; 45 left Marijke Heuff (Mr J van den Brink); 46 Ron Sutherland/Garden Picture Library (designer Murray Collins Design); 47 Georges Leveque; 48 left Michael Newton; 48 right Ron Sutherland/Garden Picture Library; 49 Marijke Heuff (Mr & Mrs de la Hayze); 50–51 Marijke Heuff (Mr & Mrs Brinkworth); 52 Lamontagne; 53 Eric Crichton; 54 Jerry Harpur (designer Barbara Wenzel); 55–56 Georges Leveque; 57 above Eric Crichton (Brook Cottage); 57 below Marijke Heuff (Mr & Mrs van Heel); 58 John Heseltine; 59 Philippe Perdereau; 60 left John Heseltine; 60 right Andrew Lawson; 62 Marijke Heuff (Mr & Mrs Peters); 63 left Elizabeth Whiting & Associates; 63 right Jerry Harpur (Stone House, Stone); 64 above Jerry Harpur (Mackenzie Bell); 64 below Eric Crichton ('The Old Rectory'); 65 Marijke Heuff (Ineke Greve); 66 Jerry Harpur; 67 Philippe Perdereau; 68 Boys Syndication; 69 Georges Leveque; 70 Marijke Heuff (Mr & Mrs Adriaanse); 71 Jerry Harpur (Sir Alexander and Lady Bethune); 72 Georges Leveque; 73 above Marijke Heuff (Mr & Mrs Groenewegen); 73 below Philippa Lewis (designer Peter Dunlop); 74 Boys Syndication; 75 John Heseltine; 76 Eric Crichton (Barnsley House); 77 Georges Leveque; 80 Georges Leveque; 81 Andrew Lawson; 82 Jerry Harpur (designer John Plummer); 85 Georges Leveque; 86 Jerry Harpur (designer Christopher Masson); 88 above Ron Sutherland/Garden Picture Library; 88 below Boys Syndication; 90 Marijke Heuff (designer Mr K T Noordhuis); 93 Steven Wooster/Garden Picture Library; 95 Gary Rogers; 100 above Marijke Heuff (Mr & Mrs Brattinga); 100 below Marijke Heuff (Mr & Mrs Berenschot); 102 left Gary Rogers; 104 Jerry Harpur (designer Richard Shelbourne); 105 Linda Burgess/Insight; 106 Marijke Heuff (Mr & Mrs Helsen); 107 above Marijke Heuff (Mr & Mrs Brinkworth); 107 below Ron Sutherland/Garden Picture Library; 108 Jerry Harpur (Sue Du Val); 108–109 Peter Woloszynski; 109 Marijke Heuff; 110 Marijke Heuff (Marte Roling); 112 Marijke Heuff (Mr & Mrs Lambooy); 113 Marijke Heuff (designer Piet Oudolf); 114 left Andrew Lawson; 114 right Philippe Perdereau; 116 left Marijke Heuff; 116 right Eric Crichton; 117 Steve Wooster/Garden Picture Library; 118 Rodney Hyett/Elizabeth Whiting & Associates; 119 Marijke Heuff (designer Mien Ruys & Hans Veldhoen); 122 Lamontagne; 124 Marijke Heuff (Mr & Mrs Hummelen); 126 Jerry Harpur; 127 David Stevens; 128 Lamontagne; 134 Lamontagne; 137 Jerry Harpur (Sue Du Val).

Special photography by Jerry Harpur: (architect John Burgee, garden Gwen Burgee with Tim Du Val) 33, 41 left, 99 (Terence and Caroline Conran) 96, 115, 120, 121 (designer Tim Du Val) 1, 14, 18 right, 78, 98 (Mrs Harry Fitzgibbons – designer Christopher Masson) 5 above left, 43, 111 (Lucy Manoff – designer Tim Du Val) 102 right (Thomas & Louise McNamee – designer Tim Du Val) 36, 79, 94 (Landscape Architect Daniel Stewart) 35, 61, 125 (Lee Wheeler – designer Christopher Masson) 37, 41 right, 91.

144